COME AND SEE

A Study on the Gospel of John

KRISTIN SCHMUCKER

Study Suggestions

We believe that the Bible is true, trustworthy, and timeless and that it is vitally important for all believers. These study suggestions are intended to help you more effectively study Scripture as you seek to know and love God through His Word.

SUGGESTED STUDY TOOLS

- A Bible

- A double-spaced, printed copy of the Scripture passages that this study covers. You can use a website like *www.biblegateway.com* to copy the text of a passage and print out a double-spaced copy to be able to mark on easily

- A journal to write notes or prayers

- Pens, colored pencils, and highlighters

- A dictionary to look up unfamiliar words

HOW TO USE THIS STUDY

Begin your study time in prayer. Ask God to reveal Himself to you, to help you understand what you are reading, and to transform you with His Word (Psalm 119:18).

Before you read what is written in each day of the study itself, read the assigned passages of Scripture for that day. Use your double-spaced copy to circle, underline, highlight, draw arrows, and mark in any way you would like to help you dig deeper as you work through a passage.

Read the daily written content provided for the current study day.

Answer the questions that appear at the end of each study day.

HOW TO STUDY THE BIBLE

The inductive method provides tools for deeper and more intentional Bible study. To study the Bible inductively, work through the steps below after reading background information on the book.

1. OBSERVATION & COMPREHENSION
Key question: What does the text say?

After reading the daily Scripture in its entirety at least once, begin working with smaller portions of the Scripture. Read a passage of Scripture repetitively, and then mark the following items in the text:

- Key or repeated words and ideas
- Key themes
- Transition words (Ex: therefore, but, because, if/then, likewise, etc.)
- Lists
- Comparisons & Contrasts
- Commands
- Unfamiliar words (look these up in a dictionary)
- Questions you have about the text

2. INTERPRETATION
Key question: What does the text mean?

Once you have annotated the text, work through the following steps to help you interpret its meaning:

- Read the passage in other versions for a better understanding of the text.
- Read cross-references to help interpret Scripture with Scripture.
- Paraphrase or summarize the passage to check for understanding.
- Identify how the text reflects the metanarrative of Scripture, which is the story of creation, fall, redemption, and restoration.
- Read trustworthy commentaries if you need further insight into the meaning of the passage.

3 APPLICATION
Key Question: How should the truth of this passage change me?

Bible study is not merely an intellectual pursuit. The truths about God, ourselves, and the gospel that we discover in Scripture should produce transformation in our hearts and lives. Answer the following questions as you consider what you have learned in your study:

- What attributes of God's character are revealed in the passage?

    Consider places where the text directly states the character of God, as well as how His character is revealed through His words and actions.

- What do I learn about myself in light of who God is?

    Consider how you fall short of God's character, how the text reveals your sin nature, and what it says about your new identity in Christ.

- How should this truth change me?

    A passage of Scripture may contain direct commands telling us what to do or warnings about sins to avoid in order to help us grow in holiness. Other times our application flows out of seeing ourselves in light of God's character. As we pray and reflect on how God is calling us to change in light of His Word, we should be asking questions like, "How should I pray for God to change my heart?" and "What practical steps can I take toward cultivating habits of holiness?"

THE ATTRIBUTES OF GOD

ETERNAL

God has no beginning and no end. He always was, always is, and always will be.

HAB. 1:12 / REV. 1:8 / IS. 41:4

FAITHFUL

God is incapable of anything but fidelity. He is loyally devoted to His plan and purpose.

2 TIM. 2:13 / DEUT. 7:9
HEB. 10:23

GOOD

God is pure; there is no defilement in Him. He is unable to sin, and all He does is good.

GEN. 1:31 / PS. 34:8 / PS. 107:1

GRACIOUS

God is kind, giving us gifts and benefits we do not deserve.

2 KINGS 13:23 / PS. 145:8
IS. 30:18

HOLY

God is undefiled and unable to be in the presence of defilement. He is sacred and set-apart.

REV. 4:8 / LEV. 19:2 / HAB. 1:13

INCOMPREHENSIBLE & TRANSCENDENT

God is high above and beyond human understanding. He is unable to be fully known.

PS. 145:3 / IS. 55:8-9
ROM. 11:33-36

IMMUTABLE

God does not change. He is the same yesterday, today, and tomorrow.

1 SAM. 15:29 / ROM. 11:29
JAMES 1:17

INFINITE

God is limitless. He exhibits all of His attributes perfectly and boundlessly.

ROM. 11:33-36 / IS. 40:28
PS. 147:5

JEALOUS

God is desirous of receiving the praise and affection He rightly deserves.

EX. 20:5 / DEUT. 4:23-24
JOSH. 24:19

JUST

God governs in perfect justice. He acts in accordance with justice. In Him, there is no wrongdoing or dishonesty.

IS. 61:8 / DEUT. 32:4 / PS. 146:7-9

LOVING

God is eternally, enduringly, steadfastly loving and affectionate. He does not forsake or betray His covenant love.

JN. 3:16 / EPH. 2:4-5 / 1 JN. 4:16

MERCIFUL

God is compassionate, withholding from us the wrath that we deserve.

TITUS 3:5 / PS. 25:10
LAM. 3:22-23

OMNIPOTENT

God is all-powerful; His strength is unlimited.

MAT. 19:26 / JOB 42:1-2
JER. 32:27

OMNIPRESENT

God is everywhere; His presence is near and permeating.

PROV. 15:3 / PS. 139:7-10
JER. 23:23-24

OMNISCIENT

God is all-knowing; there is nothing unknown to Him.

PS. 147:4 / I JN. 3:20
HEB. 4:13

PATIENT

God is long-suffering and enduring. He gives ample opportunity for people to turn toward Him.

ROM. 2:4 / 2 PET. 3:9 / PS. 86:15

SELF-EXISTENT

God was not created but exists by His power alone.

PS. 90:1-2 / JN. 1:4 / JN. 5:26

SELF-SUFFICIENT

God has no needs and depends on nothing, but everything depends on God.

IS. 40:28-31 / ACTS 17:24-25
PHIL. 4:19

SOVEREIGN

God governs over all things; He is in complete control.

COL. 1:17 / PS. 24:1-2
1 CHRON. 29:11-12

TRUTHFUL

God is our measurement of what is fact. By Him are we able to discern true and false.

JN. 3:33 / ROM. 1:25 / JN. 14:6

WISE

God is infinitely knowledgeable and is judicious with His knowledge.

IS. 46:9-10 / IS. 55:9 / PROV. 3:19

WRATHFUL

God stands in opposition to all that is evil. He enacts judgment according to His holiness, righteousness, and justice.

PS. 69:24 / JN. 3:36 / ROM. 1:18

TIMELINE OF SCRIPTURE

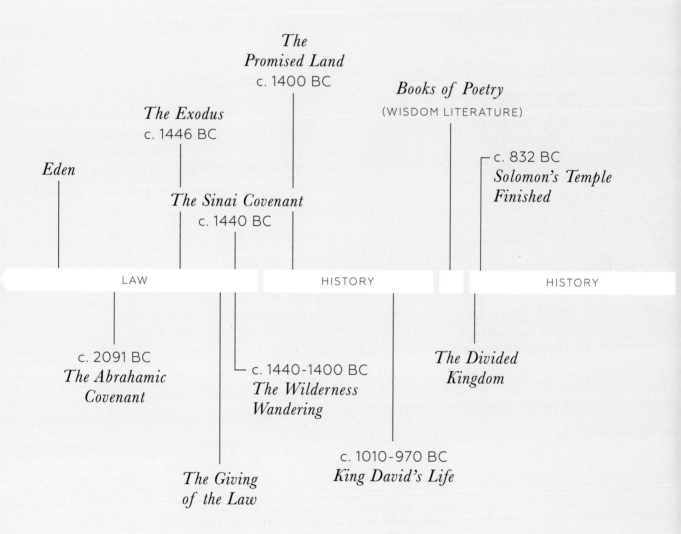

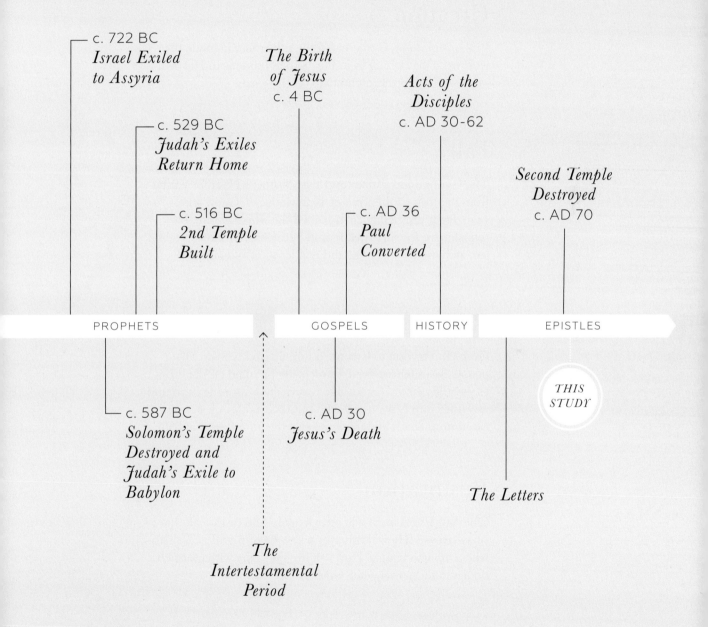

Study Suggestions / 9

METANARRATIVE OF SCRIPTURE

Creation

In the beginning, God created the universe. He made the world and everything in it. He created humans in His own image to be His representatives on the earth.

Fall

The first humans, Adam and Eve, disobeyed God by eating from the fruit of the Tree of Knowledge of Good and Evil. Their disobedience impacted the whole world. The punishment for sin is death, and because of Adam's original sin, all humans are sinful and condemned to death.

Redemption

God sent His Son to become a human and redeem His people. Jesus Christ lived a sinless life but died on the cross to pay the penalty for sin. He resurrected from the dead and ascended into heaven. All who put their faith in Jesus are saved from death and freely receive the gift of eternal life.

Restoration

One day, Jesus Christ will return again and restore all that sin destroyed. He will usher in a new heaven and new earth where all who trust in Him will live eternally with glorified bodies in the presence of God.

Table of Contents

WEEK ONE	19
SCRIPTURE MEMORY	39
WEEKLY REFLECTION	40

WEEK TWO	43
SCRIPTURE MEMORY	63
WEEKLY REFLECTION	64

WEEK THREE	67
SCRIPTURE MEMORY	89
WEEKLY REFLECTION	90

WEEK FOUR	93
SCRIPTURE MEMORY	113
WEEKLY REFLECTION	114

WEEK FIVE	117
SCRIPTURE MEMORY	137
WEEKLY REFLECTION	138

WEEK SIX	141
SCRIPTURE MEMORY	161
WEEKLY REFLECTION	162

WEEK SEVEN	165
SCRIPTURE MEMORY	185
WEEKLY REFLECTION	186

WEEK EIGHT	189
SCRIPTURE MEMORY	209
WEEKLY REFLECTION	210

WEEK NINE	213
SCRIPTURE MEMORY	233
WEEKLY REFLECTION	234

WEEK TEN	237
SCRIPTURE MEMORY	257
WEEKLY REFLECTION	258

EXTRA RESOURCES:

STUDY SUGGESTIONS	2
SCRIPTURE MEMORY SCHEDULE + HELPFUL TIPS	14
THE LAND OF ISRAEL IN NEW TESTAMENT TIMES	16
JESUS TRAVELS THROUGH SAMARIA	71
MIRACLES IN THE BOOK OF JOHN	260
SEVEN I AM STATEMENTS OF CHRIST	262
PASSION WEEK TIMELINE	264
WHAT IS THE GOSPEL?	266

The opening verses of John 1 are some of the
most beautiful verses in all of Scripture.

They tell us who Jesus is and why He came. Throughout the next ten weeks, we will be studying the book of John, and we have provided a schedule for you to memorize this beautiful prologue over the upcoming weeks. Time spent memorizing Scripture is always time well spent, and this passage will be a reminder to your heart and mind of who Jesus is.

SCRIPTURE MEMORY SCHEDULE

WEEK 1	JOHN 1:1
WEEK 2	JOHN 1:2-3
WEEK 3	JOHN 1:4-5
WEEK 4	JOHN 1:6-7
WEEK 5	JOHN 1:8-9
WEEK 6	JOHN 1:10-11
WEEK 7	JOHN 1:12-13
WEEK 8	JOHN 1:14
WEEK 9	JOHN 1:15-16
WEEK 10	JOHN 1:17-18

Helpful Tips for Scripture Memorization

- READ THE VERSE REPETITIVELY.

- MEDITATE ON THE MEANING OF THE VERSE.

- INSTEAD OF JUST MEMORIZING THE WORDS, SEEK TO ALLOW THEM TO PENETRATE YOUR HEART.

- PRAY THE VERSE.

- THINK ABOUT WHAT THE VERSE TEACHES YOU ABOUT THE CHARACTER OF GOD.

- THINK ABOUT HOW THE VERSE APPLIES TO YOUR LIFE.

- THINK ABOUT WHAT YOU KNOW FOR SURE AFTER READING THE VERSE.

- TRY WRITING OUT THE VERSE TO TEST YOUR MEMORY.

- REVIEW THE VERSES YOU HAVE MEMORIZED OFTEN TO KEEP THEM FRESH.

- KEEP THE VERSE WITH YOU THROUGHOUT YOUR DAY TO REVIEW.

- RECITE THE VERSE OUT LOUD.

- REVIEW MULTIPLE TRANSLATIONS TO BETTER UNDERSTAND THE VERSE.

- MEMORIZE THE REFERENCE AS WELL, SO THAT YOU KNOW WHERE IT IS LOCATED.

- LOOK UP DEFINITIONS OF UNFAMILIAR WORDS.

- SET THE VERSE TO MUSIC.

- MEMORIZE WITH A FRIEND, AND KEEP EACH OTHER ACCOUNTABLE.

- READ THE CONTEXT OF THE VERSE TO GET A BETTER UNDERSTANDING OF ITS MEANING.

- STUDY THE VERSE IN-DEPTH.

- LISTEN TO THE VERSE OR ENTIRE PASSAGE ON AN AUDIO BIBLE.

- HAVE FUN!

- CHALLENGE YOURSELF!

- REVIEW. REVIEW. REVIEW.

THE LAND OF ISRAEL IN NEW TESTAMENT TIMES

WEEK 1 DAY 1

> THE BOOK OF JOHN EXPLORES THE DEPTHS OF THEOLOGY IN A WAY THAT EVERY PERSON, OLD OR YOUNG, CAN UNDERSTAND.

THAT YOU MAY BELIEVE

READ: JOHN 1 - 21

MENTIONED SCRIPTURE:

John 21:20-24
John 3:16
John 15
John 17
Genesis 1

Jesus performed many other signs in the presence of his disciples that are not written in this book. But these are written so that you may believe that Jesus is the Messiah, the Son of God, and that by believing you may have life in his name.
John 20:30-31

It may seem odd to begin the introduction to a study with a passage near the end of the book, but it is in these two short verses that we find John's thesis statement for this beautiful book. The book of John is written so that we might believe.

As implied by its title, this gospel was written by the Apostle John. He identifies himself in John 21:20-24 as "the disciple Jesus loved." He was part of the inner circle and one of our Savior's closest companions on this earth. He could have given himself a great and noble title but instead chose to be identified as loved by Jesus.

The book of John is written so that we might believe.

The book of John is unique among the four Gospels. While the first three are commonly referred to as the Synoptic Gospels because of their vast similarities, John stands on its own as unique among the four. It is simple, and it is profound—so simple that it is often regarded as the starting place for someone exploring Christianity or new to the faith but so profound that the greatest scholars have not yet mined its depths.

The book of John is a call to believe. It is a call to recognize that Jesus is the Messiah. He is who He says He is. It is a call to a faith that trusts Him, not just for salvation but for every moment of our lives. It is a call to life. It is a call to the kind of life that is overflowing and abundant, which can only be found in Him.

The book overflows with themes like belief and life. It contains some of Scripture's most well-known passages like John 3:16 and some of Scripture's most comforting and encouraging passages like Jesus's call for His disciples to abide in Him in John 15 and the High Priestly Prayer in John 17. Unlike the way that some of the other Gospels begin, John does not begin with a record of birth or baptism. Instead, the book's opening words take us back to the very beginning in a way reminiscent of Genesis 1. John announces to us the genesis of a new era and a new covenant.

The book explores the depths of theology in a way that every person, old or young, can understand. It points often to Jesus's fulfillment of the Old Testament, and it explicitly states that Jesus is the Messiah and is in fact God made flesh. The book calls us to believe but not to a belief that is mere intellectual assent. It calls us to believe with every fiber of our being. It calls us to a belief that is only possible through the Spirit's work in us. It calls us to a belief that trusts God with every aspect of our lives and finds our joy in Him alone. The book calls us to abide in Christ and be transformed into His image.

Whether you have never studied the Bible before, or whether you have been studying the Bible your entire life, the book of John is for you. It is for believers and for those who have never heard the name of Jesus before. It is for the hungry, the seeking, the skeptic, the weary, and the broken. For every problem that we face, the book of John points us to one answer, and His name is Jesus.

DAY 1 QUESTIONS

1. AFTER READING THE ENTIRE BOOK OF JOHN, WHAT KEY WORDS AND THEMES STAND OUT TO YOU?

2. WHAT VERSE STANDS OUT TO YOU THE MOST? WHY?

3. WHAT DID YOU OBSERVE ABOUT THE CHARACTER OF GOD IN THE BOOK OF JOHN?

4. WRITE OUT A PRAYER ASKING GOD TO SHOW YOU MORE OF WHO HE IS THROUGH THE BOOK OF JOHN.

WEEK 1 DAY 2

> JESUS IS GOD, AND THAT CHANGES EVERYTHING.

THE WORD

READ: JOHN 1:1-5

CROSS REFERENCE:

Genesis 1
Psalm 107:20
Isaiah 38:4
Jeremiah 1:4
Isaiah 55:10-11
2 Corinthians 4:6
Isaiah 9:2
Psalm 119:105
2 Samuel 23:4

John opens this book by taking us back to the beginning. Instead of beginning with the birth of Jesus or the start of His ministry, he goes all the way back to the beginning of creation. His opening words call to mind the opening words of Genesis. He is calling our attention to a new genesis through the person of Jesus Christ. He does not leave us in suspense in declaring who Jesus is. He quickly announces that Jesus, who he calls "the Word," has been from the beginning where He was with God and that in fact, He is God in the flesh. This is the radical message that he brings. With just a few words carefully crafted into one single verse, John has placed his cards on the table. Jesus is God, and that changes everything.

The first eighteen beautiful verses of John provide a poetic prologue to the book. Inside these verses, we find a stunning declaration of who Jesus is as well as a highlight of many of the major themes of the book. And with every verse we are pointed to Jesus.

Life is found in Christ, and there is not life apart from Him.

In the very first verse, we see Jesus described as "the Word." The Greek *logos* was an important term at the time in Greek philosophy as it spoke of some higher and divine power. This understanding is helpful but not complete as we consider Jesus as the Word. John also had in mind the word of God spoken of often in the Old Testament. In Genesis 1, it is the words of God that create the world, and we are told here in the first verses of John that this is none other than the Lord Himself. The Old Testament tells us that God's word create and also that it is where salvation and deliverance are found (Psalm 107:20). And it is the word of God that spoke through the prophets (Isaiah 38:4, Jeremiah 1:4) and the word of God that has accomplishing power (Isaiah 55:10-11). God's word creates, delivers, reveals, and accomplishes. And the fullest revelation of who God is and of His word is set forth for us in Jesus.

It is from the words of Jesus that all things were created and from His word that all things hold together. Without Him, there is nothing. John emphasizes for us the importance of the man from Nazareth. By beginning with the deity of Jesus, John calls his readers to belief.

Throughout the book, John will compel his readers to believe and find life in the name of Jesus, and here he will introduce us to this theme of life. This same Jesus who has spoken light and life into this world has shone the light of the gospel into our hearts through the face of Jesus (2 Corinthians 4:6). Life is found in Christ, and there is not life apart from Him.

He is life. He is light. And His light shines and could not be overcome. The tenses of the words here are interesting to note in verse 5. "Shines" is in the present tense but "has not overcome" points us to a past event. John points out to us that the light of Jesus and His gospel shines even now, and nothing has overcome it. Though Satan and evil tried to overcome at the cross, they did not and could not succeed. Even the darkness of the cross is illuminated by the light of His glory. The darkness of sin was not too black that His love could not wash it clean. The darkness of death was not too vast that He could not overcome it. And the darkness of the tomb was not too cold and black that the light of resurrection morning could not break through.

The truth of the Word of God will drive out the darkness and illuminate the darkest shadows of our lives. The light of Jesus shines, and it is this light that reveals to those of us who were trapped in darkness the light of Christ (Isaiah 9:2). It is this light that guides God's people every step of the journey (Psalm 119:105). And it is this light that grows us to maturity in Him (2 Samuel 23:4). In the book of John, we glimpse the glory of Jesus, and when we walk away from this great Gospel, we will be forever changed.

DAY 2 QUESTIONS

1. WHAT ARE SOME OF THE THEMES OR KEYWORDS IN THIS PASSAGE?

2. THINK ABOUT THE CHARACTERISTICS OF LIGHT. WHAT DOES LIGHT DO, AND HOW IS THIS DEMONSTRATED FOR US SPIRITUALLY IN JESUS?

3. HOW DOES JOHN 1:5 GIVE YOU HOPE?

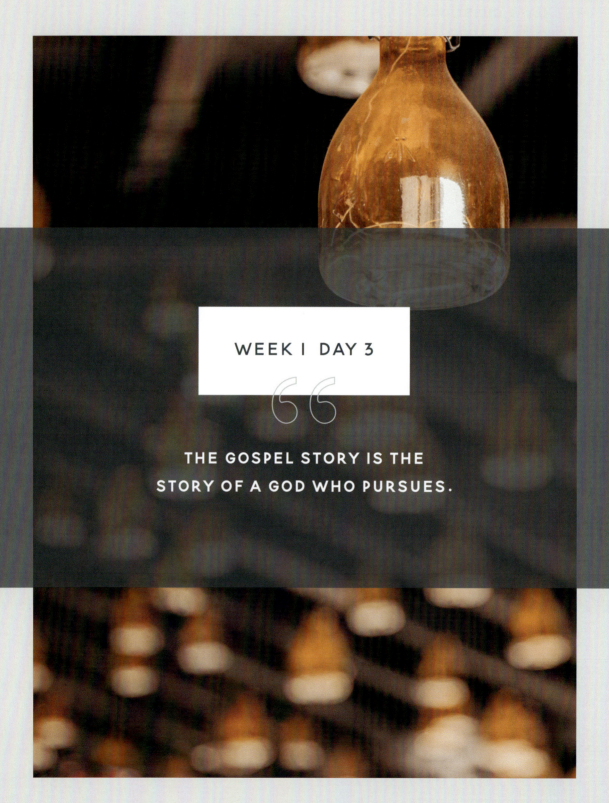

WEEK 1 DAY 3

"

THE GOSPEL STORY IS THE STORY OF A GOD WHO PURSUES.

THE TRUE LIGHT HAS COME

READ: JOHN 1:6-13

Perhaps these passages are so familiar to you that you could nearly quote them. Or perhaps this is the first time that you have ever read these words. As we study through the book of John, read slowly. Think about the weight of the words and the depth of meaning found within them. In today's passage, we are introduced to a man named John. This is not the author of the book, but instead it is John the Baptist. We are introduced to John as a man sent by God. This was a designation that placed him among the prophets. He was a man with a message, and His message was about a man who was the Messiah. He came to be a witness. He came to point to the light, and the light is Jesus.

In verse 9 we turn our eyes back to Jesus who was the substance of John's message. He is the true light. Though counterfeit lights have fought for the attention of humanity throughout history, Jesus is the true light. He is the light that pierces through our darkness. He is the light that wakes us from our sleep. He is the light that guides and directs our steps. He is the light that

He came to break through the darkness, and the world did not notice.

declares the solution to the darkness of sin in this world. And He came. He came as a baby in humility. He became a man and took on flesh. He came to break through the darkness, and the world did not notice.

He made the world through the power of His word, and yet the world did not know Him. Prophets had foretold His coming, and generations had longed for His coming, yet as this light came to the tiny town of Bethlehem, the world did not even know that it happened. Life continued as normal, even though everything had changed.

He came to His own. They should have recognized Him. He came to Israel, the people chosen by God to bring forth the Messiah, but they paid no attention. The wording here in Greek gives the idea of coming home. He came home to His own, and they should have been waiting for Him and rejoicing in His coming, and yet when He came, they did not receive Him. The glorious news of the coming of the One who created the world is met with the tragedy of rejection.

But the story that John is writing does not stay as a tragedy. He also tells us of the good news. He tells us the message of this gospel—that there would be some who would receive Him, not of their own power or strength and not because of something good inside of them but because of grace. They would believe because of the God who sought after them. Both in Jesus's day and throughout all ages, God would call a people to Himself through His power. Jesus came to bring salvation to His children. And though many rejected Him, God would open the eyes of His children to the message of grace poured out through Jesus.

The gospel story is the story of a God who pursues. It is the story of the light that breaks through the darkness of this world to ransom His sons and daughters. It is a story that points us to the cross.

May we direct our vision to the cross. May we open our eyes to His light. May we not live like those who were in the presence of Jesus, acting like He was not there. May we live in the truth that He has come and He is with us. May we too be witnesses of the light.

DAY 3 QUESTIONS

1. READ THE DESCRIPTION OF JOHN THE BAPTIST IN JOHN 1:6-8. IN WHAT WAYS SHOULD THIS DESCRIPTION BE A DESCRIPTION OF ALL BELIEVERS?

2. WHAT DO THESE VERSES TEACH YOU ABOUT GOD'S CHARACTER?

3. HOW DOES THIS PASSAGE ENCOURAGE YOU TO PRAISE GOD?

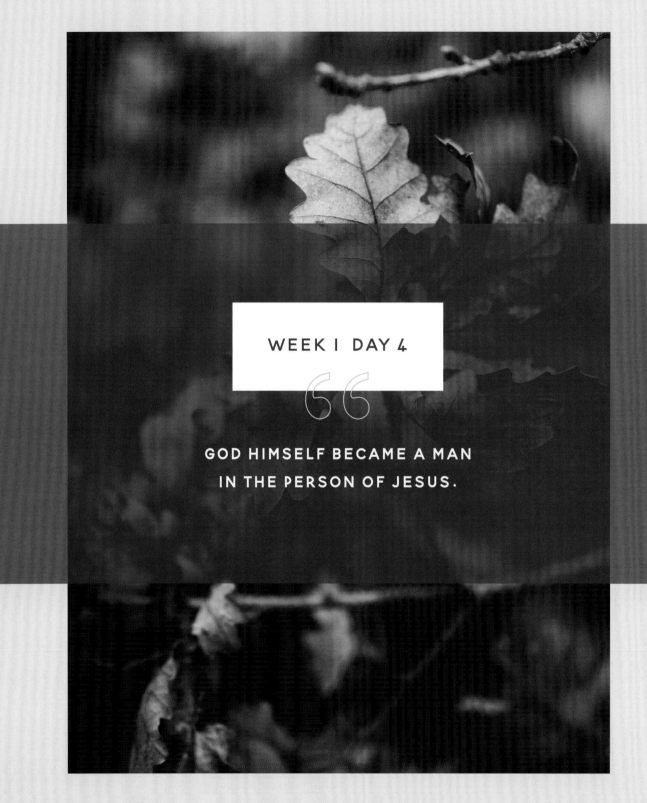

THE WORD BECAME FLESH

READ: JOHN 1:14-18

CROSS REFERENCE:

Exodus 33 – 34

Exodus 34:6-7

John concludes his majestic prologue with today's passage. The very first verse of the book of John introduced us to the eternal Word, and now John gives us a shocking revelation that should leave us in wonder and awe no matter how many times we have read these words. The Word became flesh. God Himself became a man in the person of Jesus. The eternal, immortal Son of God took on humble flesh. He came into a stable in Bethlehem. He was born of a lowly peasant girl, born in poverty, and born because of His love for His own.

John 1:14 not only tells us that He became flesh but that He came to dwell among us. The Greek word here literally means that He pitched His tent. The word would have instantly drawn the minds of John's readers to another important dwelling place with the same name—the tabernacle. We could literally read this verse to say that "He tabernacled among us." He pitched His tent on this earth. And just as the tabernacle of the Old Testament was humble and unassuming on the outside, so was He. But there was more to the tabernacle than met the eye. It was the dwelling

> In Jesus, we see the glory of God. And this glory is full of grace and truth.

place of God. It was where God dwelt among His people. In a new way, Jesus was the dwelling place of God. In Him was the glory of God. He broke through the mundane with His magnificent presence and drew near to His people.

In Jesus, we see the glory of God. And this glory is full of grace and truth. Again, John is drawing His readers back to the Old Testament. The description of Jesus would have reminded the people of Exodus 33-34. It is in this passage that Moses asks to see God's glory and is told that God is abounding in steadfast love and faithfulness (Exodus 34:6-7). Though these words have been translated in a variety of ways, their meaning is nearly identical to John's declaration of Jesus as full of grace (God's covenant steadfast love), and truth (God's faithfulness to the truth of His Word). And the glory, grace, and truth of who Jesus is would soon be displayed in its fullest measure at the cross.

This Jesus was the One to whom John was pointing. And in Him, we receive grace upon grace. From Him, grace overflows, and in Him is the only place that true grace is found. The grace that is found in Him is inexhaustible. Martin Luther said, "This fountain is inexhaustible; it is full of grace and truth before God; it never fails no matter how much we draw from it…It remains a perennial fount of all grace and truth, an unfathomable well, an eternal fountain. The more we draw from it, the more it gives." This well never runs dry, and for the child of God, every moment is overflowing with the grace that only He can give.

Verse 17 points us to the law. The law was good, but it had no power to save a fallen humanity. It pointed us to our need, but because we could never keep it, it had no power to save. But grace and truth come from Jesus alone. In fact, many of the descriptions of Jesus throughout the book of John such as being light, truth, bread, and living water are also used to describe the law. We are seeing Jesus as the fulfillment of the law. The gracious, unmerited favor of God flowed down in drops of blood on the cross of Calvary. And the truth of God was affirmed in every promise kept and every promise fulfilled. In Jesus, we find all that we need.

John ends His prologue by reminding us that no man has ever seen God face to face—until now. As we look on the face of Jesus and as we see His works, we see God. We see who He is and what He does. We see grace like a river and mercy fall like rain on our parched and thirsty souls. But Jesus has made Him known to us. The phrase "made Him known" is the Greek *exegesato*. It is the word from which we get "exegete" or "exegesis." Bible scholars use this word when they talk about studying the Bible and knowing what the Bible means. But here we are told that Jesus has made God known to us. It is explained through Him. Our eyes our opened to the character and goodness of God as we see Jesus. And when we see Jesus, our lives will never be the same.

DAY 4 QUESTIONS

1. TAKE A MOMENT TO THINK ABOUT THE TRUTH THAT GOD BECAME A MAN TO RESCUE HIS PEOPLE. WHAT STANDS OUT TO YOU THE MOST ABOUT THE MIRACLE OF GOD BECOMING A MAN?

2. JESUS IS DESCRIBED AS FULL OF GRACE AND TRUTH. WHAT DOES THIS TEACH YOU ABOUT HOW WE SHOULD RESPOND TO OTHERS IN GRACE AND TRUTH?

3. IN WHAT WAYS DOES JESUS REVEAL THE FATHER TO US?

WEEK 1 DAY 5

> BOTH JEW AND GENTILE WOULD FIND FREEDOM IN THE MATCHLESS GRACE OF JESUS.

BEHOLD, THE LAMB OF GOD

READ: JOHN 1:19-34

CROSS REFERENCE:

Isaiah 40:3

Exodus 12

In today's passage, we are given a glimpse into the life and ministry of John the Baptist. As John was preaching, the Jews sent priests and Levites to inquire who he was and what exactly he was doing. John made it very clear that he was not the Messiah, Elijah, or the prophet who was to come. But, though he did not claim to be the Messiah, he did make a very startling statement by quoting Isaiah 40:3 and claiming to be the fulfillment of that prophecy of one crying in the wilderness to point to the Messiah. John was a messenger, and his message was Jesus.

When John spoke of Jesus, he spoke of One who was not recognized among His own people, and John emphatically stated that he was not even worthy to remove the sandals from Jesus's feet. This reference gives us great insight to what John was trying to communicate to those who listened to his words. In the first-century culture, people walked everywhere. When you combine foot travel with dirty and dusty desert roads and a culture that wore sandals, the people's feet would get dirty very quickly. Sandals would be removed when entering a home, but this task was re-

"Behold, the Lamb of God, who takes away the sin of the world!"

served for the lowest of servants. Only Gentile servants would perform such a disgusting task. Yet when the highly respected John compares himself to Jesus, he tells those listening that he is not worthy to do even the lowest task for the Messiah. He was brilliantly illustrating the honor of Jesus and the humility that our posture should be before Him.

We are invited in to one particular moment in John's ministry right before he baptizes Jesus. Jesus was walking toward him, and John said, "Behold, the Lamb of God, who takes away the sin of the world!" It was a radical declaration. For the Jews listening in, it was a new way of referring to the Messiah. And yet, these words had a very clear meaning. The sacrificial lamb was one of the most prominent themes in all of the Old Testament Scriptures. Most markedly, the lamb was the key symbol found in the Passover in Exodus 12. The blood of the lamb would be the covering of the people of God and would set them free from bondage. John was announcing that the true Lamb had come, and He too would cover the sins of His people and set them free from their bondage of sin. But unlike the original Passover lamb that was primarily for the Hebrew people, this Lamb of God would come to offer salvation to the entire world. Both Jew and Gentile would find freedom in the matchless grace of Jesus.

John proclaimed the message of the perfect, spotless, Lamb of God. He pointed to the Son of God incarnate. His life and ministry were like a neon sign pointing to the Promised One. Every promise of the Old Testament would be fulfilled in the true Lamb, the true Prophet, and the Messiah. On the dusty streets of Galilee, John proclaimed the greatest message that had ever been. God Himself had become flesh. He had come to dwell in the midst of His people. He had come to save. The blind would see, and the deaf would hear. Chains would be broken, and those once lost in darkness would see the Light of the world break through the darkness.

John's life pointed to Jesus, and this should be our prayer for our own lives as well. Like John, we can recognize our unworthiness but marvel in His grace upon grace in calling us to Himself. What a gift to do even the most menial tasks for the glory of His name. May every moment of our lives point to His grace and proclaim the goodness of the gospel.

DAY 5 QUESTIONS

1   WHAT CAN YOU LEARN FROM HOW JOHN THE BAPTIST POINTED TO JESUS?

2   READ EXODUS 12 AND MAKE SOME OBSERVATIONS ABOUT THE SIGNIFICANCE OF JESUS BEING CALLED THE LAMB OF GOD.

3   WHAT DO YOU LEARN ABOUT GOD'S CHARACTER FROM THIS PASSAGE?

WEEK 1

SCRIPTURE MEMORY

JOHN 1:1

In the beginning was the Word, and the Word was with God, and the Word was God.

WEEK ONE REFLECTION

REVIEW
John 1:1-34

PARAPHRASE THE PASSAGE FROM THIS WEEK.

_____
_____
_____
_____
_____
_____
_____

WHAT DID YOU OBSERVE FROM THIS WEEK'S TEXT ABOUT GOD AND HIS CHARACTER?

_____
_____
_____
_____
_____
_____
_____
_____

WHAT DOES THIS WEEK'S PASSAGE REVEAL ABOUT THE CONDITION OF MANKIND AND YOURSELF?

_____
_____
_____
_____
_____
_____
_____

HOW DOES THIS PASSAGE POINT TO THE GOSPEL?

_____
_____
_____
_____
_____
_____
_____
_____

HOW SHOULD YOU RESPOND TO THIS PASSAGE? WHAT SPECIFIC ACTION STEPS CAN YOU TAKE THIS WEEK TO APPLY THIS PASSAGE?

_____
_____
_____
_____
_____
_____
_____
_____
_____

WRITE A PRAYER OF RESPONSE TO YOUR STUDY OF GOD'S WORD.

Adore God for who He is, confess sins that He revealed in your own life, ask Him to empower you to walk in obedience, and pray for anyone who comes to mind as you study.

_____
_____
_____
_____
_____
_____

WEEK 2 DAY 1

> JOHN BEAUTIFULLY SETS FORTH A NEW CREATION STORY AND INVITES US TO SEE THAT THIS STORY OF JESUS IS THE SAME STORY OF THE ONE WHO CREATED THE WORLD.

FOLLOW ME

READ: JOHN 1:35-51

CROSS REFERENCE:

Genesis 1

Exodus 4:22

Deuteronomy 1:31

Jeremiah 31:20

Hosea 11:1

2 Samuel 7:14

Psalm 2:7

Genesis 28:10-22

John 14:6

As we move into the ministry of Jesus, we see Jesus calling the first disciples. We also can begin to see a pattern emerging in John 1 where we see a new creation narrative being written for us. As John 1 echoes the beginning lines of Genesis with, "In the beginning," we also see a sequence of days at the opening of Jesus's ministry much like the creation narrative. John beautifully sets forth a new creation story and invites us to see that this story of Jesus is the same story of the One who created the world.

In this description of the calling of the first disciples, we also see many names of Jesus. The book of John is full of names of Jesus, and we can see that clearly in the first chapter of John's Gospel. We have already seen Jesus given many titles including: the Word, the Creator, life, and light, in the earlier verses of the chapter. Here in verse 36, John the Baptist again refers to Jesus as the Lamb of God and continues to show that Jesus is the true Passover Lamb that would be sacrificed for the sins of His own. We also see Jesus called Rabbi, which means "teacher." The disciples would learn from Jesus, their great teacher, and be transformed by His great gospel. Even the word "disciple" signifies them as students or learners under the master teacher.

The good news of the gospel is that He is everything we are seeking.

Andrew was quick to share this life-changing news with his brother, Peter. And when he tells Peter about Jesus, he exclaims that they had found the Messiah or the Christ. Though these men did not fully comprehend all that it meant that Jesus was the long-awaited Messiah, they knew that this was the One who they had been waiting for—all of Israel had been waiting and hoping for. This is further enforced for us when Phillip tells Nathanael that this Jesus is the one of whom Moses, the Law, and the Prophets spoke. He was radically stating that all the hopes of Israel were hinged on this man. This carpenter's son who would next be called Jesus of Nazareth and the son of Joseph was the One who God's people had waited and prayed for. God was answering the prayers of generations in the most unexpected way, and as Jesus opened the eyes of the disciples and found them, He calls for them to follow Him.

The narrative moves quickly as we see ordinary men meet Jesus. Soon we see Jesus identified as the Son of God. This was a term that had been applied to the nation of Israel in the Old Testament (Exodus 4:22, Deuteronomy 1:31, Jeremiah 31:20, Hosea 11:1), and as the story of redemption began to unfold throughout the Old Testament, it began to be clear that the true son of God would be one man (2 Samuel 7:14, Psalm 2:7). Jesus is the true Israel. He is what Israel could never be: the true chosen and anointed Son of God. Jesus is also identified here as the King of Israel and the Son of Man. Little by little, the fullness of who Jesus is was being revealed to these new followers, and they were compelled to tell others about Him.

The final verses of today's passage point back to the Old Testament. Verse 51 may not seem to make sense to us at first, but Jesus was speaking to Jewish men who would have been very familiar with what he was sharing. Jesus was referencing the events of Genesis 28:10-22 when Jacob was on the run from Esau. He was weary, discouraged, and far from God. But God came to Him and met him where he was. God confirmed His covenant and bridges the gap between heaven and Earth with a ladder. Jesus is telling us here that He is that ladder. Jesus is the One who brings heaven to Earth by coming to redeem us. Jesus is the ladder that brings us to God. He is the way, the truth, and the life, and the way that we are brought near to the Father (John 14:6). Jesus bridges that gap and brings us near.

As the disciples are introduced to Jesus of Nazareth, everything changes. Jesus asks them what they are seeking and gives the call to follow Him without reservation. The same question is asked of all of us as we come to the book of John and see Jesus. What are we seeking? What need are we looking for Him to fill? What ache in our hearts do we wonder if He can heal? The good news of the gospel is that He is everything we are seeking. Every longing is fulfilled in Him, and all that we seek is found in Jesus.

DAY 1 QUESTIONS

1. MAKE A LIST OF ALL THE NAMES OR TITLES OF JESUS FOUND IN TODAY'S PASSAGE. YOU CAN ALSO GO BACK AND ADD OTHER NAMES FOUND EARLIER IN CHAPTER 1.

2. JESUS ASKED THE DISCIPLES WHAT THEY WERE SEEKING. WHAT WOULD YOUR ANSWER BE? WHAT ARE YOU SEEKING FROM JESUS? WHAT DO YOU NEED FROM HIM?

3. NOTICE THAT THE RESPONSE OF THE DISCIPLES WHEN THEY MEET JESUS IS TO GO AND TELL OTHERS ABOUT HIM. IS THIS YOUR NATURAL RESPONSE? HOW CAN YOU GROW IN SHARING CHRIST WITH THOSE AROUND YOU THIS WEEK?

WEEK 2 DAY 2

"

WE CAN TAKE HEART THAT JESUS' TRANSFORMING POWER IS WITH US. IT IS WORKING IN WAYS WE MAY NOT SEE AND MOVING IN WAYS WE MAY NOT UNDERSTAND.

NEW WINE

READ: JOHN 2:1-12

CROSS REFERENCE:

Isaiah 1:18

John 10:10

Revelation 19:6-8

John 2 begins a new section in the book of John as well as beginning the public ministry of Jesus. John 2-12 are often referred to as the Book of Signs because of the strong emphasis in these chapters on the miracles of Jesus. It is in today's reading that we witness the first public miracle of Jesus. At first glance, we may wonder what exactly the point of this particular miracle was. But as we dig a little deeper and see both the cultural context and the religious context in which it took place, we begin to see the message that this first miracle was meant to convey. And its message is for us as well as the original audience.

The scene picks up for us at a wedding in Cana. Jesus, His mother Mary, and His disciples are in attendance. Immediately, we see Mary coming to Jesus to tell Him that the wine had run out. This may seem insignificant to us, but in the culture of the day, this would be a mark of shame on the family that was expected to show hospitality to their guests. But on this day, Jesus would show that His transforming power could erase shame and make way for a new covenant.

The transforming power of Jesus is the overarching message of this situation.

Mary came with a problem, and though Jesus instructed that His hour had not yet come, in faith, she instructed the servants to do whatever He told them to do. In their obedience, they would take part in His miracle. Jesus used what was available—six water jars used for purification rituals. The meaning of what He did was not an accident. When He commanded the servants to fill the jars, He wanted them filled to the brim. The servants were commanded to take some of this water to the master, and when he tasted it, it was the greatest wine. The wine was so good that it was noted that the good wine is usually served first and then replaced by something inferior. But Jesus did something different and something new. The most ordinary substance had been transformed by Jesus.

The transforming power of Jesus is the overarching message of this situation. But looking a little deeper, we can learn so much from this event. Jesus used the water jars designated for purification. The jars held water meant to cleanse and purify the outside of a man or woman, but Jesus was bringing a new way. He came to be the One who would purify His people, but not simply by changing their actions or cleansing their exterior. Jesus came to cleanse from the inside out. He came to make hearts that were as white as snow (Isaiah 1:18). The old system of cleansing was done away with, and a new way had come. A better way had come because Jesus had come. And all the symbols of the Old Testament laws would find their fulfillment in Him.

Another common theme seen in Jesus's miracles and in this one as well is the extravagant grace of Jesus. He could have made just enough to get by, but instead, the pots were overflowing with the very best wine. He erased the shame of not enough with overflowing and abundant refreshment. Later in the book of John, Jesus would say that He had not only come to give life but to give abundant life (John 10:10). This new way was not just a way to get by; it was a way of overflowing life and peace that is found in Jesus alone. It is the way that shame is erased and hope is found. In this miracle, Jesus's glory was revealed as verse 11 tells us. His power over all things and His grace toward humanity are seen in His tender concern for the smallest of details. And the result is belief. This is what John will point us to over and over again. The things that Jesus did and said caused people to believe, for in Him, they saw the face of God. God had come near to dwell among men, and nothing would ever be the same.

So Jesus's ministry begins with a wedding just as the book of Genesis also opened with a wedding. But the good news for God's people is that all of creation is moving toward another wedding where Jesus is the groom and the church is His bride (Revelation 19:6-8), and on that day we will feast on the wine of His presence as we worship our Savior. On that day free from sin, and with tears and death forever in the past, we will proclaim, "He has saved the best wine until now."

As believers today, we can take heart that Jesus's transforming power is with us. It is working in ways we may not see and moving in ways we may not understand. Our shame is gone. No longer do we need to work to earn His favor; He has showered His favor on His sons and daughters. And His provision is sweet and overflowing. It reaches every part of our brokenness and extends its healing flow to every part of our hearts. New wine has come. His glory has been revealed. Now we must believe in Him.

DAY 2 QUESTIONS

1 MARY'S INITIAL RESPONSE WAS TO GO TO JESUS WITH HER CONCERN. WHERE DO YOU GO WITH WORRIES, ANXIETIES, SITUATIONS, AND CONCERNS?

2 OVER THE NEXT FEW CHAPTERS, WE WILL LOOK AT MANY OF JESUS' MIRACLES. WHAT DO YOU THINK THE PURPOSE OF JESUS' MIRACLES WAS? DOES JOHN 2:11 SHED LIGHT ON THEIR PURPOSE?

3 WHAT DO YOU LEARN ABOUT THE CHARACTER OF JESUS FROM THIS MIRACLE? HOW DOES IT ENCOURAGE YOU IN YOUR OWN LIFE?

WEEK 2 DAY 3

JESUS CAME TO CLEANSE.

CLEANSE US

READ: JOHN 2:13-25

John is very concerned that we know who Jesus is, believe on His name, and find life in Him. To many, Jesus's cleansing of the temple seems out of place with the other accounts in the Gospels. It is here that we see a righteous anger for the glory of God and the worship of the Lord from Jesus. It is important as we approach this passage that we focus on the heart issues that Jesus was seeking to address. This will give us insight into what our own response should be to this passage.

During Passover, the Jews would take their pilgrimage to Jerusalem to worship and offer sacrifice. It was a time of remembering how God had delivered them from the bondage of slavery in Egypt. It was a treasured time of worship and celebration. When Jesus arrived in the temple, He found that the outer court of the Gentiles had been transformed into a mercantile. The temple court was bustling and busy with trade. Merchants and money changers had set up shop in the midst of the temple.

> It is important that we focus on the heart issues that Jesus was seeking to address.

They were selling animals for sacrifice and changing currency for offerings. Jesus does not rebuke them here for the selling of animals or the exchanging of money. These things were in fact necessary for those traveling from afar. Animals would need to be purchased, and currency would need to be exchanged. But God sees the heart. Jesus was looking past the surface level, concerned with a deeper problem.

The people had turned the holy temple into a place of spiritual consumerism. Many thought they were doing the right thing by coming to worship, but they had made it all about themselves. The place that should have been set aside for worship was transformed into a place of convenience and ease for the worshipers at the expense of the worship of God. The tables were likely set up right in the midst of the court of the Gentiles. This meant that Gentiles would have no place to worship. It is probable that the outcasts were pushed out for the convenience of the "in crowd." Worship had become about what was comfortable and easy instead of being about true worship of a holy God.

Jesus would not stand for it. His zeal for the glory of the Father caused Him to drive out those who had made worship about themselves instead of about the Lord. This passage is usually titled as the cleansing of the temple, and it follows the theme of cleansing found in the passage preceding it. Jesus came to cleanse. The cleansing of the temple was the duty of the priest, and as Jesus entered the temple that day, He was establishing Himself as a true and better priest who would bring cleansing that was not just momentary and external, but lasting and eternal.

The Jews demanded a sign from Him. They wanted Jesus on their own terms, but He would not give in. Jesus knew their hearts. Instead, He spoke of a sign to come. If they would destroy the temple, He would raise it up in three days. They scoffed and mocked. But what they did not realize, and what even the disciples did not realize until after the resurrection, was that He was not speaking of the stone temple that stood before them. His resurrection from the grave would be the greatest sign. He was speaking of His own body. His body was the temple come to Earth. His flesh and blood were the way that He tabernacled among man and bridged the gap between God and humanity. Heaven had come down in Him. They wanted a sign, but He wanted to give them Himself.

The final verses of the chapter again draw our attention to Jesus's perception of what was happening in the hearts of those around Him. He was not fooled by the lip service of those who said they believed. He knew that the masses did not want Him; they wanted what He could do for Him. They did not want transformation and cleansing; they wanted signs and wonders. He knew their thoughts, and He knew their hearts because He was their God.

This passage has great application for us as we live in a consumer culture that also focuses on what we can get from God, instead of focusing on God Himself. Jesus came for cleansing. He did not come to perform signs and work miracles to satiate our temporary desires. He came to transform hearts and cleanse from sin. He came to make us new. He knows our hearts. He knows when we worship our preferences above God. He knows when we demand signs instead of trusting His sovereignty. And yet, He calls us to Himself. He comes to cleanse and make us new. He calls us to love Him and believe in Him, not just for what He can do for us but because of who He is. He gives us Himself, and there is no greater gift.

DAY 3 QUESTIONS

1. WHAT DO WE LEARN ABOUT JESUS FROM THIS PASSAGE?

2. WHY DO YOU THINK JESUS WAS SO UPSET ABOUT WHAT WAS TAKING PLACE IN THE TEMPLE?

3. WHAT CAN YOU LEARN FROM THIS PASSAGE THAT APPLIES TO YOUR OWN LIFE?

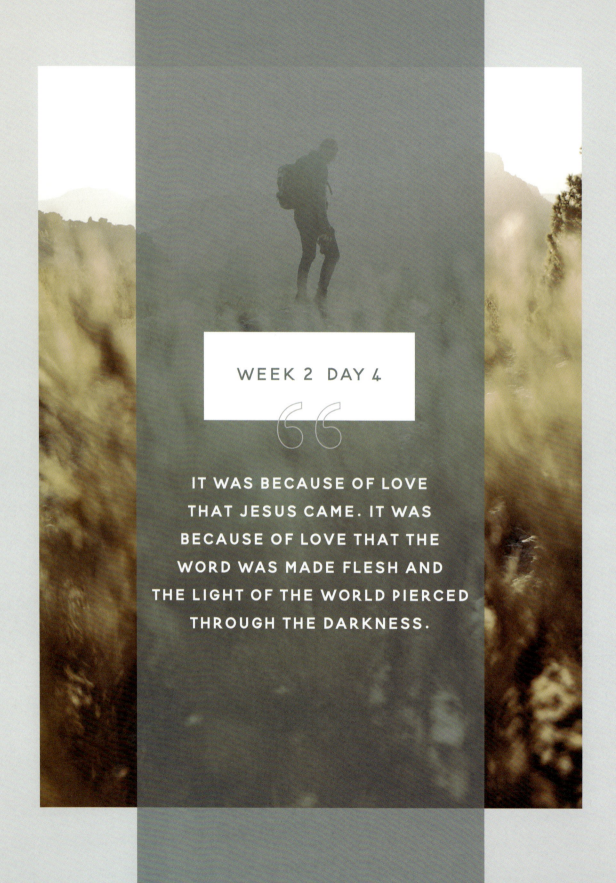

WEEK 2 DAY 4

> IT WAS BECAUSE OF LOVE THAT JESUS CAME. IT WAS BECAUSE OF LOVE THAT THE WORD WAS MADE FLESH AND THE LIGHT OF THE WORLD PIERCED THROUGH THE DARKNESS.

YOU MUST BE BORN AGAIN

READ: JOHN 3:1-21

CROSS REFERENCE:

Ezekiel 36:25-27
Numbers 21:4-9
John 3:16
Romans 8:35-39

It is in this passage that we find some of the most well-known words in all of Scripture. Seeing the context in which Jesus spoke the famous words about the love of the Father and the gift of the Son in John 3:16 only deepens our appreciation for this verse. It is in this passage that we are introduced to a man named Nicodemus and told that he was a Pharisee and a ruler of the Jews. He comes to Jesus at night. He is curious about this great teacher and recognizes that Jesus has been sent from God. Jesus's words to Nicodemus were a striking declaration that he must be born again. Though Nicodemus knew the Old Testament and followed the law, he had missed how it spoke of Jesus in every verse, and he did not understand what Jesus meant. Nicodemus and the rest of the religious elite had focused on external righteousness, but God wanted to give His people new hearts (Ezekiel 36:25-27). Jesus shifted his gaze from the external to the internal.

He has drawn us to Himself.

The phrase, "born again," confused Nicodemus. He questioned if a man needed to crawl back into his mother's womb to be born again. But Jesus was speaking of a spiritual birth, not a physical birth. And this spiritual birth was not of the will of man but of the will of God. Jesus pointed to the wind that was perhaps blowing in the trees as he spoke to Nicodemus. The wind blows, but you cannot see it. It is real and working, but we do not control it. So too is salvation the work of the Spirit that works and moves in ways that we cannot see or understand. In ourselves, we could not even muster the faith to believe, but the Spirit has given us new hearts and a new birth. He has drawn us to Himself.

Jesus pointed Nicodemus to the Word of God and an event that took place in the book of Numbers where a serpent was lifted up for the salvation of God's people (Numbers 21:4-9). Jesus said that He Himself would be lifted up, and all who believe would find life in His name. It is the message of John spoken to a man in the middle of the night. It is the message that will run from the first verse to the last. Believe on the name of Jesus.

Then comes the most famous verse. John 3:16 has been called, "the Bible in miniature," by Martin Luther. In this short verse, we see the plan of God and the story of redemption. It was because of love that Jesus came. It was because of love that the Word was made flesh and the Light of the world pierced through the darkness. And as Nicodemus stood in the darkness of night under the darkness of sin, he looked in the eyes of the Light of the world. God so loved the world, that He gave. He gave His Son to display to the world what love is. He gave what we needed. He gave Himself in the form of a man.

It is interesting to note that the word "loved" is in the past tense. God did not love us when we started loving Him. He loved us before the foundations of the world. He loved us while we stumbled in our sin and groped in darkness. He loved us when we were far from Him, and He brought us near through the power of the Spirit. Jesus did not come to condemn. We were already condemned because of the sin of our first parents. He came to save. He came to redeem. He came so that we could be born again.

The sadness of this passage is that many would reject Him, hate Him, and eventually kill Him. But their wickedness would not catch God off guard. He knew about that too. The Son of man would be lifted up to die, and yet still He came to redeem His own.

These verses should remind us of the glory of salvation. They should cause us to rejoice in the love and faithfulness of our God. They should remind us of the gift of Jesus and the joy of life in Him. Romans 8:1 reminds us that for those in Christ, there is no condemnation. Those whom He saves will never be condemned. And Romans 8:35-39 reminds us there is nothing and no one that will ever separate us from the love of God that has been poured out to us through Jesus. We are His if we believe in His name.

DAY 4 QUESTIONS

1. WHAT DO WE LEARN ABOUT GOD FROM THIS PASSAGE? WHAT DO WE LEARN ABOUT OURSELVES?

2. HOW DO YOU THINK JOHN 3:16 DISPLAYS THE MESSAGE OF THE WHOLE BIBLE?

3. TO WHAT HOPE FROM THIS PASSAGE CAN WE CLING?

WEEK 2 DAY 5

"

HE MUST INCREASE.
I MUST DECREASE.
THIS IS THE CRY OF A DISCIPLE.

HE MUST INCREASE, BUT I MUST DECREASE.

READ: JOHN 3:22-36

The third chapter of John ends by shifting our attention back to John the Baptist and showing us how John sought to point all attention to Jesus. This was the purpose and goal of His life, and we are wise to follow his example and learn from his words.

As Jesus and the disciples went out into the Judean countryside teaching and baptizing, a discussion arose between John and an unnamed Jew. This is a dispute or an argument taking place over a jealousy that seems to have been rising up in the followers of John. John had come preparing the way for the Lord. He came to preach the message of repentance and point to the spotless Lamb of God. He came to announce the coming of Jesus. But somewhere along the way, some of his followers sensed the spotlight shifting off of John and onto Jesus as Jesus began to minister publicly.

John's life and words pointed to Jesus as the only One worthy of glory, honor, and worship.

John's response reveals the heart of his ministry and the attitude that all followers of Jesus should have. John points his followers again to Jesus and reminds them that this is what God had called him to do. John uses an illustration that was commonly used in the Old Testament prophets. He uses a wedding to symbolize the relationship between Jesus and His disciples just as the illustration was used of God and Israel in the Old Testament and would be used of Christ and the Church in the New Testament. John tells his followers that he is only the groomsman. He is the friend of the groom or the best man. His duty is simply to assist the groom. The glory is not his own. John knew that his job was not to build a following but to point all who would hear his message to the One whom they should follow.

John's famous words echo out as an anthem that we should also live out. He must increase. I must decrease. This is the cry of a disciple.

As we read the discourse that took place, we can see the way that John explained these poignant words. He explains why Jesus is better, and in doing so, he pours out praise for Jesus. The first reason that John gives is that Jesus is from above and above all. He was telling those listening in that day that Jesus was so much more than a man. Jesus was God made flesh. He then told the people that Jesus was sent by the Father to speak the words of God. Because Jesus is God, the words that He spoke were the words of God. His words are far greater than the words that any person, including John, could speak. Jesus came with the words of life. Finally, John explained that Jesus had authority over all things because the Father had given all things into His hand. John's life and words pointed to Jesus as the only One worthy of glory, honor, and worship.

The passage ends with a reminder of the message of the gospel that this third chapter of John has proclaimed throughout. All who believe in the Son receive eternal life, but the wrath of God falls on those who reject Him. Those who reject Christ continue in their condemned state, but there is life and hope for those who believe in the Son and the message of His gospel.

We can learn many things from this account. In it we are reminded that our human tendency is to want our own glory. We seek to build our own names, our own fame, and our own followings. But the purpose of a Christian is never to build his or her own name but to magnify His name. We live to point to Jesus. These words cause us to evaluate our own hearts and the ways that we have sought our own glory. They also remind us that we must never place loyalty to a human leader above loyalty to Christ. Humans will let us down. Jesus never will. So then, we must live to make Him known. We must seek His glory. We must humble ourselves and come in worship before the Son of God and the Savior of the world.

"We can never make too much of Christ…We can never have too high thoughts about Christ, can never love Him too much, trust Him too implicitly, lay too much weight upon Him, and speak too highly in His praise. He is worthy of all the honor that we can give Him. He will be all in heaven. Let us see to it, that He is all in our hearts on earth."

J.C. RYLE

DAY 5 QUESTIONS

1. WHAT CAN WE LEARN ABOUT SERVING GOD FROM THIS ACCOUNT?

2. IN WHAT WAYS ARE WE TEMPTED TO SEEK OUR OWN GLORY INSTEAD OF THE GLORY OF CHRIST?

3. WHAT SHOULD MOTIVATE US TO SERVE THE LORD? WHAT ARE SOME FAULTY MOTIVATIONS?

WEEK 2

SCRIPTURE MEMORY

JOHN 1:2-3

He was with God in the beginning. All things were created through him, and apart from him not one thing was created that has been created.

WEEK TWO
REFLECTION

REVIEW
John 1:35 – 3:36

PARAPHRASE THE PASSAGE FROM THIS WEEK.

WHAT DID YOU OBSERVE FROM THIS WEEK'S TEXT ABOUT GOD AND HIS CHARACTER?

WHAT DOES THIS WEEK'S PASSAGE REVEAL ABOUT THE CONDITION OF MANKIND AND YOURSELF?

HOW DOES THIS PASSAGE POINT TO THE GOSPEL?

HOW SHOULD YOU RESPOND TO THIS PASSAGE? WHAT SPECIFIC ACTION STEPS CAN YOU TAKE THIS WEEK TO APPLY THIS PASSAGE?

WRITE A PRAYER OF RESPONSE TO YOUR STUDY OF GOD'S WORD.

Adore God for who He is, confess sins that He revealed in your own life, ask Him to empower you to walk in obedience, and pray for anyone who comes to mind as you study.

WEEK 3 DAY 1

" JESUS IS WHO WE LONG FOR.
JESUS IS WHAT WE NEED.

LIVING WATER

READ: JOHN 4:1-26

CROSS REFERENCE:

Jeremiah 2:13

Jesus is the one for whom we long. Jesus is who we need. He is the answer to our brokenness, our sin, and our shame. No matter who you are, where you have been, or what you have done, Jesus is the only One who will satisfy. In chapter 3, we were introduced to Nicodemus. He was a highly respected religious leader. Here in chapter 4, we are shown a contrast as we meet the woman from Samaria. She is totally different than Nicodemus, and yet Jesus brings the same message that the gospel is for all. Whether rich or poor, young or old, prestigious or outcast, there is only one answer to the aching in our souls—Jesus is the answer to our brokenness, no matter what form it takes.

The message of Jesus had begun to spread to the Jews, but in these verses, we see the gospel go to the Gentiles as well. As chapter 4 opens, Jesus had been making disciples throughout Judea. Now He sets out for Galilee, and the text tells us that He had to pass through Samaria. A quick glance at a map shows that Samaria seems like the most likely route to get from Judea to Galilee, but in

Jesus had an appointment at Jacob's well, and He would not miss it.

first century culture, there would have been many religious Jews who would have shunned this route. The Samaritans were hated by the Jews. They were viewed as outcasts and half-breeds. The racism and prejudice ran deep, especially for the most religiously elite. But Jesus said that this was the way He must go. The words seem to show more than just the fastest possible route, and more about His intention to go to Samaria. He had an appointment at Jacob's well, and He would not miss it.

Jesus sat down next to Jacob's well around noon as the heat of the sun beat overhead when a woman came to draw water from the well. This was not the typical time to draw water. Water was most often drawn in the early morning to stay out of the scorching sun. We are not told why she came at this time of day. Perhaps it was to escape the scornful looks of the other women who came to draw, or perhaps it was because unbeknownst to her, she also had an appointment at Jacob's well.

The woman was shocked when Jesus (a Jewish man), asked her (a Samaritan woman) for a drink. These things were not done. Jewish men did not talk to women, and they definitely did not speak publically to Samaritan women. This was socially taboo on many levels. Jesus's reply to her shock was a life-changing offer. He offered her living water—water that would cause her to never thirst again. Her mind raced. If she had this water, she would never be thirsty again. If she had this water, she would never have to come to this well again. She would never have to feel the look of shame from those around her. When Jesus asked her to call her husband, her shame had been exposed. We are told that she had five husbands and that the one who she was currently living with was not her husband. We are not given many more details. Was her shame because of something she had done? Had she lived a life of immorality? Or was her shame because of something that had been done to her? In a culture where divorce was nearly entirely the prerogative of the male, perhaps she had been caught in a cycle of pain that was not her own doing. Regardless, she was left with shame. But Jesus knew. He saw her pain and her brokenness, and He declared that there was a solution.

Her thoughts shifted to worship. Should people worship in Jerusalem like the Jews said or at Mount Gerizim like the Samaritans taught? But Jesus pointed her to a greater truth. God was more concerned with the heart of the worshiper than the place of worship.

Jesus revealed to this Samaritan woman that He was the Messiah. He was the Promised One. He was the hope who had come to rescue the world—and to rescue her. Though she would have never come to Him on her own, Jesus went after her. The appointment at Jacob's well would change her entire life.

The call to drink of the living water is one that goes out to each of us. We all look for things in this world to satisfy us. We look for something to quench our thirsty souls. But Jesus is the only One who truly satisfies. The thirst in our souls can be quenched only by His love and grace. Hope for our brokenness is found in Him. The water of this world will always leave us parched and empty. We need living water. And living water is found only in Jesus.

Apart from Jesus, we are all just broken cisterns trying to hold water (Jeremiah 2:13). We are searching anywhere for satisfaction. We are seeking lives of self-sufficiency, but the water runs right out like a glass filled with cracks. But Jesus offers a better way. In simple faith, He calls us to drink the living water that He extends to us. He calls us to Himself. He calls us to find satisfaction and rest for our souls that can only be found in His name.

DAY 1 QUESTIONS

1   WHAT DO YOU LOOK FOR TO SATISFY YOUR THIRST? WHAT DOES YOUR LIFE REVEAL THAT YOU BELIEVE WILL GIVE YOU SATISFACTION?

2   WATER IS USED AS A PICTURE THROUGHOUT SCRIPTURE, AND HERE IN THE BOOK OF JOHN, JESUS DECLARES THAT HE IS THE LIVING WATER. LOOK UP THESE VERSES IN THE OLD TESTAMENT, AND RECORD ANY OBSERVATIONS ABOUT THE PICTURES OF WATER:

   JEREMIAH 2:13

   PSALM 36:9

   ISAIAH 12:3

   ISAIAH 44:3.

3   HOW IS JESUS THE ANSWER TO OUR SHAME, SIN, AND BROKENNESS?

Jesus said,
"Everyone who drinks from
this water will get thirsty again.
But whoever drinks from the
water that I will give him
will never get thirsty again.
In fact, the water I will give him
will become a well of water springing
up in him for eternal life."

"Sir,"
the woman said to him,
"give me this water so that
I won't get thirsty and come
here to draw water."

JOHN 4:13-15

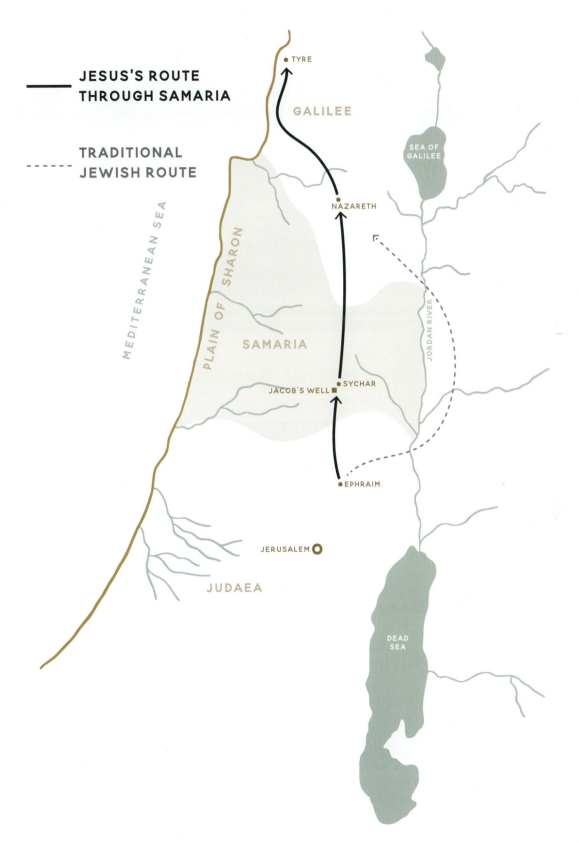

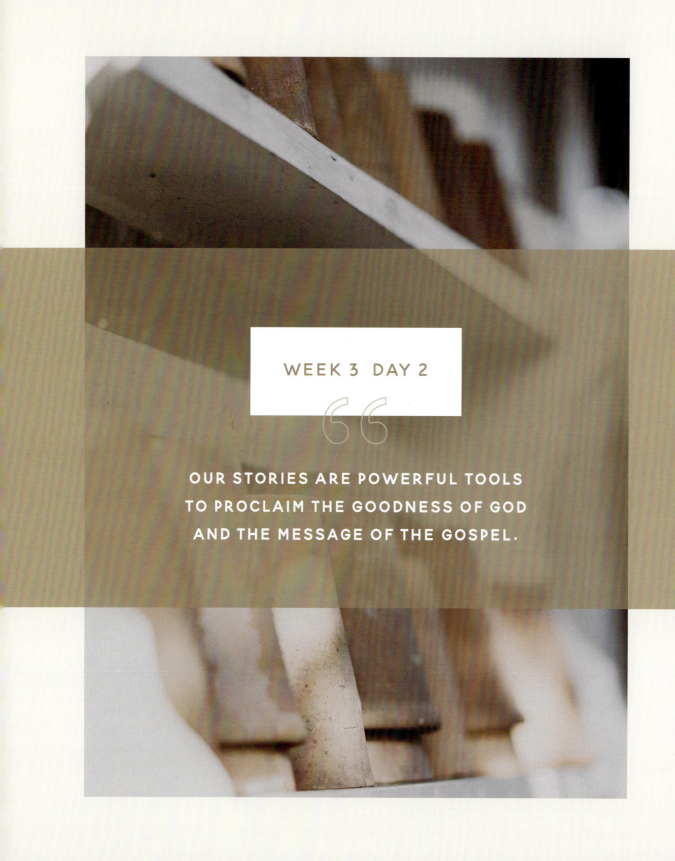

WEEK 3 DAY 2

> OUR STORIES ARE POWERFUL TOOLS TO PROCLAIM THE GOODNESS OF GOD AND THE MESSAGE OF THE GOSPEL.

SAVIOR OF THE WORLD

READ: JOHN 4:27-42

Salvation had come to the Samaritan woman, and through her testimony she would point others to the One who saves. Her story reminds us that our stories are powerful tools to proclaim the goodness of God and the message of the gospel.

The disciples returned to find Jesus speaking to this woman of Samaria, and they were shocked. You would think that they would get used to Jesus doing things differently after He turned water to wine and cleansed the temple, but it seems they were surprised every time He did something outside the normal way of doing things. This time, Jesus is not just speaking to a woman, but she is a Samaritan woman. The prejudices of the disciples ran deep. This was their culture. This was how things were done. Jewish men did not speak to women in public, they did not speak to Samaritans, and they most definitely did not speak to Samaritan women. But Jesus was not like other men. While the disciples were blinded by their prejudices and worried about appearances, Jesus was concerned with people.

The thirst of her soul had been satisfied in Jesus.

Despite the disciples' shock at the situation, they held their tongues and did not question Jesus's ways, though in their hearts the questions swirled. Just like that, the woman was gone. She left so quickly that she left her water jar behind. Perhaps the jar left behind was symbolic of her old search. She no longer was searching for something to quench her thirst; the thirst of her soul had been satisfied in Jesus. She had a message to tell to anyone who would listen: *Come and see.* It is the call of the gospel. It is a call that is seen throughout Scripture. A call to come, see, know, and experience the grace and love of God. This was her message, and the people were coming to see the man of whom she spoke.

In the meantime, the disciples urged Jesus to eat. But He had something greater on His mind than lunch. Jesus was a man. He needed physical food. But He was demonstrating for His disciples a spiritual principle. The souls of men and women were far more important than physical food. And true satisfaction comes from obeying the Father. Jesus wanted them to sense the urgency of the gospel. Jesus had come into the world, and something had changed. People were coming to Him. The kingdom was growing. And Jesus was inviting them to be a part of it. The Samaritans did not seem like the most likely converts, and yet the Samaritan woman is the first clear example of conversion in the book of John. And through her witness, many more were coming to Jesus. Jesus did not want the disciples to miss what was right in front of them. God was at work, even if it was not what they had expected.

The testimony of the Samaritan woman made the townspeople want to know this man. They saw her life, and then they came to Him. They wanted to know more based on what they had seen from her. The text makes it clear that they did not believe because of her testimony but because they came and learned who He was for themselves. Her testimony made them curious, and God used it to draw many to Himself. Their hearts now tasted the goodness of the God who they saw in her. The Samaritan people recognized that He was the Savior—not just of the Jews and not just of the religious elite—He, indeed, was the Savior of the world.

This passage should point us to the urgency of the gospel. God is working, and He is inviting us to be a part of what He is doing. He is drawing men, women, and children to Himself, and He invites us to share in His mission. Our transformed lives, like the life of the Samaritan woman, can point those around us to Jesus. Our stories do not have the power to save, but they do have the power to draw people to want to know more about who Jesus is. The Samaritan woman's story should remind us that the gospel is for all kinds of people, even the ones who seem unlikely from our limited perspectives. Let us lift our eyes and see how He is working. Let us lift our hearts in prayer and ask for Him to move. Let us lift our hands and join Him in His work.

DAY 2 QUESTIONS

1. THE DISCIPLES WERE SURPRISED THAT JESUS WAS MINISTERING TO A SAMARITAN WOMAN. WHEN WE ARE THINKING OF PEOPLE TO SHARE THE GOSPEL WITH, WHAT TYPES OF PEOPLE IN OUR OWN CULTURE AND CONTEXT DO WE SOMETIMES OVERLOOK?

2. HOW IS THE SAMARITAN WOMAN AN EXAMPLE TO US?

3. WHO IS IN YOUR LIFE THIS WEEK THAT YOU CAN SHARE YOUR STORY WITH AND POINT TO JESUS? ASK THE LORD TO GIVE YOU AN OPPORTUNITY TO SHARE THE HOPE OF JESUS WITH THAT PERSON.

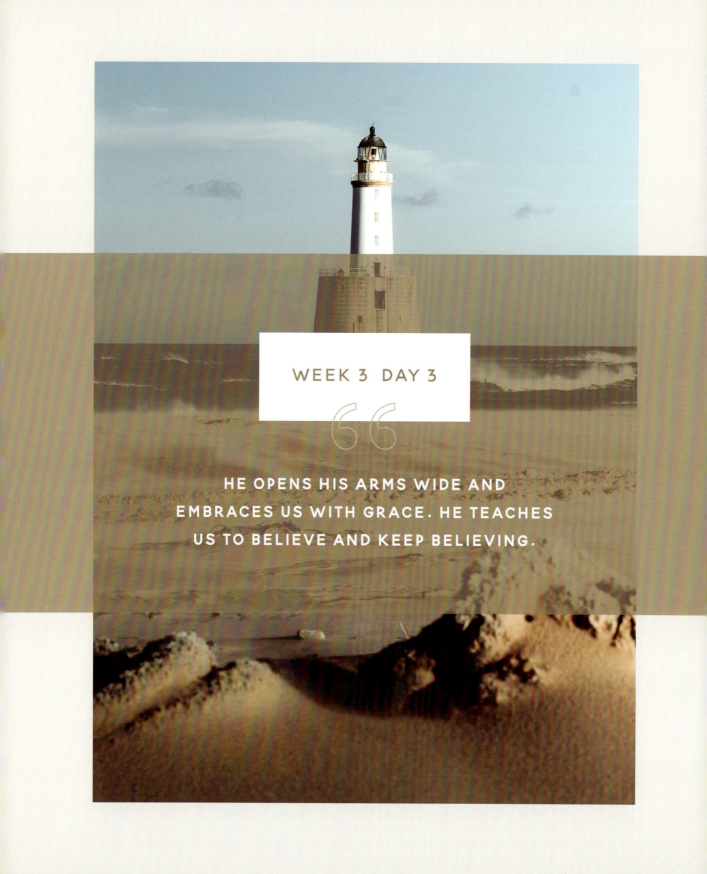

WEEK 3 DAY 3

"

HE OPENS HIS ARMS WIDE AND EMBRACES US WITH GRACE. HE TEACHES US TO BELIEVE AND KEEP BELIEVING.

BELIEVE AND KEEP BELIEVING

READ: JOHN 4:43-54

This passage is within the section in John that has been called The Book of Signs. It contains so many of the miracles that Jesus performed during His public ministry. There were some who saw Jesus only as a miracle-worker, but He is so much more than that. The man who worked miracles was also the promised Messiah and the hope of all the world. John's Gospel calls us to believe, and this account does the same.

Jesus came back to where His ministry started—back to Cana of Galilee where He had turned water into wine. In Capernaum, there was a man who came with a request for healing. This royal official was desperate for hope. His son was ill and was about to die. He knew that Jesus could heal him, so he asked for Jesus to come. Jesus's initial response may leave us confused. He says the people do not believe unless they see signs and wonders. Many were becoming intrigued by this man from Galilee. They wanted to see His miracles, but they had no interest in seeing Him as the Promised One for whom they had waited. Was this man different?

Would we still want Him if we received none of those things?

We are not told what thoughts were racing through the man's mind at that very moment, but in boldness, he chose to ask again. We can almost hear the desperation in his voice as he lifts up his plea one more time. Jesus replied with tenderness to the persistence of the man. Jesus told him to go home. His son would live. Jesus neither answered exactly the way the man had expected nor did He do exactly what he asked, but the text tells us that the man believed the word of Jesus.

When the man started his journey home, he did not even make it all the way back when his servants met him with the news. His son was recovering from his illness. He was going to be okay. The man who had already believed asked when it happened, though by the very fact that he asked the question, it seems that he already knew. The boy had been healed the same hour that Jesus had declared it to be true. The man's response was again belief.

This story teaches us far more than the events of a specific healing. It teaches us about the character of Jesus and about the faith that He desires His followers to have. Jesus pointed out the crowd's desire for signs and wonders, and in doing so, He was revealing their lack of true faith. The people wanted what He could do for them; they did not want Him. This should cause us to ask ourselves what our own lives demonstrate in this regard. Do we want all the things that we think we will get if we follow Jesus? Or do we want Him? Would we still want Him if we received none of those things? What about if we lost everything?

It is interesting to note in the passage that we are told two separate times that the man believed. He believed the words of Jesus, and He believed when He found them to be fulfilled. This points us to a significant truth. Faith is not something that happens simply at the moment of conversion. Faith is something that encompasses every moment of the Christian life. The children of God have believed the Word of God, but they are also believers who day by day cling to the Lord and trust in His ways. And just like this royal official, sometimes Jesus answers our requests in a way that is unexpected or is not exactly what we had in mind. Faith chooses to trust Him even when life does not turn out as planned. Faith chooses to trust Him when the answer does not make any sense. Faith chooses to trust Him instead of our own plans.

Jesus is full of compassion and mercy. His heart is moved by our affliction. He knows how difficult it is for us to face the unknown. He cares about our circumstances, and He cares about our hearts. He tenderly teaches us to trust Him. He teaches us to want Him more than we want the benefits that He provides. He opens His arms wide and embraces us with grace. He teaches us to believe and keep believing.

DAY 3 QUESTIONS

1   THINK ABOUT THE OFFICIAL IN THE STORY. WHAT EMOTIONS DO YOU THINK HE WAS FEELING AS HE CAME TO JESUS THAT DAY?

2   WHAT DO WE LEARN ABOUT JESUS IN THIS PASSAGE?

3   WHAT DO YOU WANT MOST IN THIS LIFE? DO YOU WANT JESUS OR JUST WHAT HE CAN DO FOR YOU? REFLECT HONESTLY BELOW ABOUT AREAS IN YOUR LIFE WHERE YOU ARE TEMPTED TO WANT THINGS YOUR OWN WAY. ASK GOD TO CULTIVATE A DESIRE FOR HIM IN YOUR HEART.

WEEK 3 DAY 4

"

THERE ARE MANY STORIES BUT ONE JESUS WHO REACHES OUT TO THOSE IN NEED WITH LOVE AND COMPASSION.

DO YOU WANT TO BE HEALED?

READ: JOHN 5:1-18

As the Gospel of John continues, Jesus continues to heal. There were some who came to Him asking for healing, but there were others like the man in this account who did not even know who He was when He healed them. There are many stories, but one Jesus who reaches out to those in need with love and compassion.

It was at the time of one of the Jewish feasts when Jesus walked by the pool of Bethesda. The pool was one that was known as a place of healing. Legend had it that the water would stir, and the first person to enter the water would be healed. For the paralyzed man who we are introduced to in these verses, the legend of healing seemed far out of reach. He had no one to help him into the water, and his limitations meant that he would never be the first to enter the healing pool. Yet there must have been some glimmer of hope in his heart for healing, because there he was by the waters. He had been an invalid for 38 years. With each passing year, the hope of healing would have realistically faded little by little.

But then came Jesus.

But then came Jesus. Jesus knew the exact number of days the man had been sick. He knew the details of his condition. He knew the pain in his heart and the cynicism that was setting in after years of disappointment. Jesus looked at the man and asked him if he wanted to be healed. The man's answer seems to have a hint of sarcasm from being jaded by life's circumstances. To the man, the answer was obvious. Of course he wanted to be healed, but he did not have any help. His situation felt hopeless. But Jesus was going deeper with His question. Healing would be a big change for a man who had been sick for so long. Did he want to give up the life of a beggar? Did he want to start anew? Did he want everything to change? Jesus told him to take up his bed and walk, and instantly he was healed. The words that flowed from the mouth of Jesus gave life to his fragile body.

As the scene shifts to the religious leaders of the day, we may expect rejoicing over this man's healing. But that is not what we see. The response of these so-called religious leaders reveals what their religion is all about. Instead of rejoicing over healing, they are immediately accusing the man of sin. Their charge is that he is violating the Sabbath by carrying his bed. It is important to note that nowhere in Scripture was there a command against carrying one's bed on the Sabbath. Instead, the religious leaders were holding the man to the impossible standards of their own man-made rules. They cared more about their own legalistic rules than they did about God's holy and gracious law.

They were not just upset at the man for carrying his bed on the Sabbath; they were also upset at Jesus for healing on the Sabbath. Jesus's response to them would only anger them more. Jesus was there doing the work of His Father. Jesus had not broken God's law, but everything about Him was an affront to the legalistic religion of the Jewish leaders. Their empty religion cared more about appearances than it did about the souls of people made in the image of God, and Jesus would not tolerate this false religion. They were perverting the good and righteous law of God to serve their own interests and secure their power. And so, they sought to kill Jesus. A man who claimed God as His Father was claiming to be God Himself, and despite the evidence of the truth of His deity, they refused to believe.

This passage has important application for our own lives. Jesus knows. He knows who we are. He knows what we are facing. He knows the pain that is a part of our stories, and He knows just how long it has been a part of our stories. He comes near to us in our brokenness when no one else does. He also asks us the hard question of if we want to be healed. Following Jesus has a cost. For the disciples, it cost them their reputations, their comfort, and ultimately their lives. The cost of following Jesus may be different for each of us, but we must know that following Jesus will cost us everything as we lay our lives down as living sacrifices. But the cost of following Jesus is always worth it. The healing that He gives reaches to every part of us. It heals what is broken and hidden. It heals what no one else can see. This passage reminds us that God is concerned with the truth of His Word and the hearts of His people. He calls us to holiness that is rooted in who He is, not the man-made rules of legalistic religion. He wants us to be holy as He is holy. He wants us to have compassion like He has compassion. He wants us to be like Jesus.

DAY 4 QUESTIONS

1   WHAT DOES IT COST TO FOLLOW JESUS?

2   WHY DO YOU THINK THAT THE RELIGIOUS LEADERS WERE SO UPSET?

3   WHAT DO WE LEARN ABOUT JESUS IN THESE VERSES?

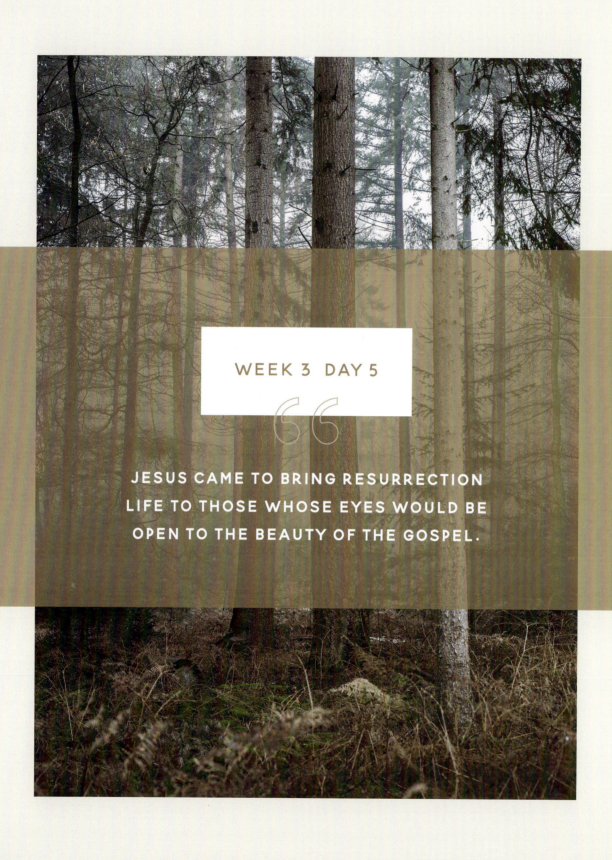

WEEK 3 DAY 5

"

JESUS CAME TO BRING RESURRECTION LIFE TO THOSE WHOSE EYES WOULD BE OPEN TO THE BEAUTY OF THE GOSPEL.

EVERYTHING POINTS TO JESUS

READ: JOHN 5:19-47

CROSS REFERENCE:

Daniel 7:13-14

After healing a man on the Sabbath, Jesus had just made the stunning declaration that God was His Father. The religious leaders knew what He was claiming. Jesus of Nazareth was claiming to be God made flesh. The words that followed were spoken directly to the religious leaders who sought to kill Him for the claims He was making.

Jesus spoke plainly to those who watched Him. His message was that the Father and the Son are one. They work in tandem along with the Holy Spirit in the mystery of the Trinity. They do not have separate wills but one unified and perfect will. The Trinity is at work in the world bringing about the plan of redemption to all who would believe. Jesus came to bring resurrection life to those whose eyes would be open to the beauty of the gospel.

This message confronted the religious leaders, and it confronts every person who comes face to face with Jesus. Is Jesus who He says that He is? The Bible does not present Jesus as merely a good teacher or a kind man who we should seek to emulate. Scripture presents Jesus as God Himself in human form. And if Jesus is God, that changes everything. These religious leaders

The authority of Jesus is the authority of God the Father.

wanted to say that they believed in God, but they were choosing to reject the One who God had sent to bring redemption. If the Father and the Son are one (and they are), then rejecting the Son was also rejecting the Father. Jesus wanted these religious people to grasp the truth of His message. God had come not to bring a religious experience but to make relationship possible between God and man.

The authority of Jesus is the authority of God the Father. John demonstrates this by using the term "Son of Man," which is found in Daniel 7:13-14. This would have caught the attention of the religious leaders who knew the Old Testament well. But Jesus did not stop there. He went on to list the witnesses to who He was. As if Jesus Himself was on trial, He lists forth those who support His case, and the evidence is irrefutable. He first speaks of John the Baptist. John had been the one who had come before, making way for the Lamb of God. He preached of the Messiah who was to come. The people of the day flocked to John's message. They wanted a deliverer. But when Jesus came, He was not what they had expected. This revealed more about their hearts than they realized. They wanted a rescuer on their terms. They wanted a God who would do things their way. But Jesus was not what they expected.

Jesus continues with the list of witnesses and points to His works. The miracles He had performed were declaring His deity and pointing to the truth of who He was. The healing that He brought physically was a sign of the healing that He had come to bring spiritually. The next witness was the Father Himself. Jesus had been sent by the Father into the world.

Jesus then pointed to the witness of the Scriptures. The religious leaders knew Scripture well. They could pull out every rule and law. They had much of the Old Testament memorized. But Jesus makes a shocking statement—in all of their study of Scripture, they had missed the point. They had searched the Scriptures because they believed that following the law was where eternal life would be found, and yet in their searching, they had missed that every verse, in every chapter, on every page, points to Jesus. It was Scripture that was bearing witness to who Jesus is. From the law that revealed a need for a Savior, to the Old Testament pictures that pointed to a redeemer, to the prophecies of the One who would come, and every verse in between, Scripture was declaring the message of Jesus. But these men, stuck in their religiosity, had missed it all. They sought the praise of men instead of the praise of God. Jesus reminded them that they thought that the law would save them, but the law, which was signified by Moses, would be the thing that would actually condemn them. They were entrenched in a life of legalism and trying to achieve their way to eternal life when Jesus stood with outstretched arms of grace, offering Himself as the way, the truth, and the life.

Christians today may read these words and think that they do not apply to them, but these words speak truth to believers as well. Like the religious leaders and the followers of John the Baptist, we are prone to imagine a god who is what we want him to be. We are sometimes shocked (though we may hide it well), that Jesus call us to humility and sacrifice. We feel surprised when we are called to suffer as He suffered. We do not want to wait. We do not want to trust. We want things the way we want them. But the gospel calls us to a different way. The gospel calls us to radical trust. It calls us to a life of waiting and resting in Him instead of living in our own strength. And though it goes against our very human tendencies, it is actually a very good thing. There is freedom to be found when we understand that the gospel is not about what we have done but about what Christ has done. It is not about all the things that we do for God but about what Jesus has done for us.

DAY 5 QUESTIONS

1. HOW IS JESUS DIFFERENT THAN WHAT THE RELIGIOUS LEADERS AND PEOPLE OF JESUS' DAY EXPECTED?

2. IN WHAT WAYS DO WE TRY TO MAKE JESUS WHAT WE WANT HIM TO BE INSTEAD OF CONFORMING OURSELVES TO WHO HE IS?

3. READ LUKE 24:13-35. HOW DOES THIS HELP YOU UNDERSTAND HOW ALL OF SCRIPTURE POINTS TO JESUS?

WEEK 3

SCRIPTURE MEMORY

JOHN 1:4-5

In him was life, and that life was the light of men. That light shines in the darkness, and yet the darkness did not overcome it.

WEEK THREE REFLECTION

REVIEW
John 4:1 – 5:47

PARAPHRASE THE PASSAGE FROM THIS WEEK.

WHAT DID YOU OBSERVE FROM THIS WEEK'S TEXT ABOUT GOD AND HIS CHARACTER?

WHAT DOES THIS WEEK'S PASSAGE REVEAL ABOUT THE CONDITION OF MANKIND AND YOURSELF?

HOW DOES THIS PASSAGE POINT TO THE GOSPEL?

HOW SHOULD YOU RESPOND TO THIS PASSAGE? WHAT SPECIFIC ACTION STEPS CAN YOU TAKE THIS WEEK TO APPLY THIS PASSAGE?

WRITE A PRAYER OF RESPONSE TO YOUR STUDY OF GOD'S WORD.

Adore God for who He is, confess sins that He revealed in your own life, ask Him to empower you to walk in obedience, and pray for anyone who comes to mind as you study.

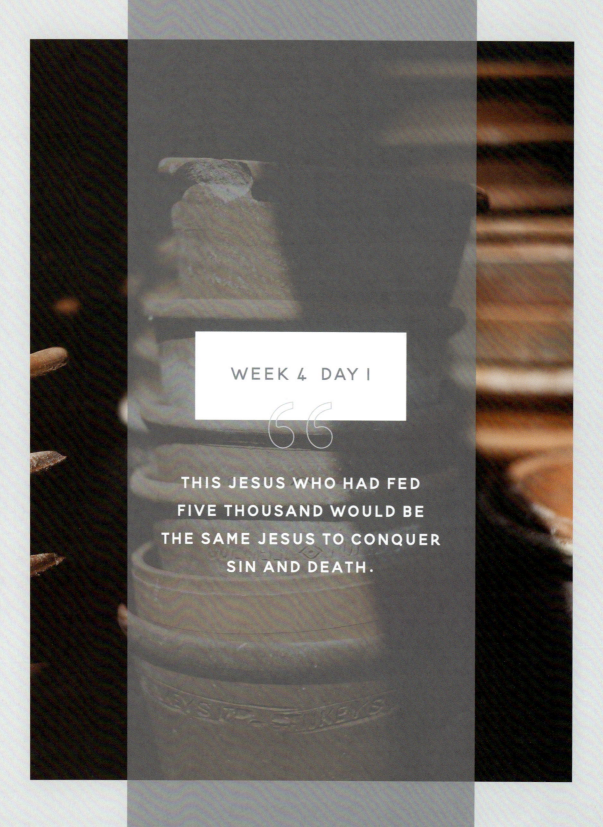

WEEK 4 DAY 1

> THIS JESUS WHO HAD FED FIVE THOUSAND WOULD BE THE SAME JESUS TO CONQUER SIN AND DEATH.

SUSTAINER

READ: JOHN 6:1-21

CROSS REFERENCE:

Deuteronomy 18:15

Chapter 5 ended with an emphasis on how the people revered Moses. It was the time of Passover, and the people were remembering their history and the deliverance of God's people out of Egypt. In chapter 6, Jesus performs miracles to show who He is, and part of what He is showing in this chapter is that He is the Promised One from long ago. He is the true and better Moses. As the Jews were in the midst of the Passover season, these pictures would have jumped out to them immediately. This miracle is also notable because it is the only miracle that appears in all four of the Gospels. This miracle shouts out the message of the gospel, that there is nothing impossible for Jesus. There is nothing that He cannot overcome.

John presents Jesus to us as the true and better Moses. He is the One Moses was pointing toward. The account begins with Jesus leading a crowd of people and going up on a mountain during the Passover season. Jesus spoke to a people enslaved like their ancestors before them, except this time their enslavement is by Rome while living in their own land. Their hearts were crying out for a deliverer, and as rumors spread around town about Jesus, many were beginning to wonder if He might be that deliverer. In the exodus, God had provided bread from heaven in the manna that was given to the people, and the miracle that would happen on this day would show a very similar provision.

> There is nothing impossible for Jesus.
> There is nothing that He cannot overcome.

The people were gathering around Jesus when He asked the disciples what they could feed them. From a human standpoint, the situation seemed impossible. The disciples were poor men who had left all to follow Jesus. They certainly did not have the money to provide food for thousands of people. Philip expressed the reality of the situation. Andrew stepped up with faith, but it was a shaky faith at best. There was a little boy with just five small loaves (we would probably call them biscuits) and two small fish. It was a little boy's lunch, not enough to feed a crowd. Andrew told Jesus of the lunch, but the reality of the situation sunk in when he asked if such a small amount would do any good. One biscuit per thousand men was hardly enough to satisfy the hunger of the crowd.

But the little was placed in the hands of Jesus. This lack of provision was no match for the great provider. The people were able to take as much as they wanted. The food did not run out. And while in Moses's day, no leftovers were allowed to be stored, in this account we see twelve baskets overflowing with plenty. There was no situation too difficult for Him to overcome. This Jesus who had fed five thousand would be the same Jesus to conquer sin and death. This is the prophet who would be like Moses who had been promised so long ago (Deuteronomy 18:15). Immediately, they wanted to make Him their king. They wanted a king who would set them free from Rome, but Jesus had come to set them free from the sin of their own hearts.

Just a few hours later, Jesus would show His power again. The disciples were in a boat when the storm began to rage around them. It was dark, and Jesus was not there. Had He forgotten them? But then they saw someone. They saw Jesus. He was walking on the water. Jesus had power over the sea. As Moses had crossed the Red Sea, Jesus was now walking on water. He had not forgotten them. He demonstrated His power yet again to their wavering hearts.

There is nothing that Jesus cannot overcome—no obstacle is too great, and there is no barrier that He cannot cross. Later in chapter 6, we will learn that Jesus Himself is the Bread of Life. He is the sustenance that we need. He is the One who sustains us, and what He provides is overflowing and abundant. We lack nothing when we have Him. Just like the disciples, our faith is shaky and unstable. But Jesus has power over the very thing that feels so uncertain to us. The waves that scared the disciples submitted to Jesus. We rest in this sovereign God who controls all things and does not leave us alone in our need. He meets us in our doubt and our wavering. He comforts us when we struggle to trust. He reminds us of who He is.

DAY 1 QUESTIONS

1 WHAT DOES THIS PASSAGE TEACH US ABOUT WHO JESUS IS?

2 WHY DOES THIS PASSAGE BRING COMFORT?

3 IN WHAT AREA OF YOUR LIFE DO YOU NEED TO TRUST GOD TO PROVIDE?

WEEK 4 DAY 2

"

HE DID NOT COME TO PROVIDE TEMPORARY DESIRES BUT TO SATISFY THE DEEPEST NEEDS OF THEIR HEARTS.

THE BREAD OF LIFE

READ: JOHN 6:22-59

CROSS REFERENCE:

Romans 8:35-39

Jesus had fed thousands with just a small lunch. He had displayed His power, and now He would magnify Jesus's provision. The people were seeking signs. They wanted to see miracles. They wanted to be fed with bread from heaven. But Jesus was showing them something more. He did not come to give physical bread but to give Himself. He did not come to provide temporary desires but to satisfy the deepest needs of their hearts. Our bodies are perpetually hungry and perpetually craving something. In the same way, our hearts and souls are forever seeking after satisfaction. Jesus comes with a message that there is One who satisfies the longings of our soul. He is the water that leaves us forever satisfied. He is the bread that leaves us forever full.

The people came asking questions. How did Jesus get to Capernaum? Jesus knew why they were there. They wanted more miracles. They wanted to feast on physical bread that He provided. But instead of answering the questions that they asked, Jesus answered the questions of their hearts. He could see past the surface

This passage calls us to hunger and thirst for Jesus.

of their words to the most inner workings of their hearts. He told them to seek not after what perishes but what is eternal. Their instinct was to ask how they could work for it. What must they do? Jesus's answer was shocking. Instead of giving them a list of laws to keep or a list of things to do to be considered a good person, Jesus tells them to believe in Him who was sent from God. Their response was to ask for a sign. They reminded Jesus of Moses and the continuous manna in the wilderness. Jesus's response was that a new manna had come.

It had not been Moses who had provided manna but God Himself. And the same God who provided manna in the wilderness had sent Jesus to be the Bread of Life. He is the water that quenches the thirsty soul. He is the bread that satisfies the hungry. And the satisfaction that He gives is not for a moment but for eternity.

The answer to their deep need was to believe in Him. Life is found in His name. The hungry and thirsty are satisfied in Him alone.

But the people did not rush to Him in faith that day. Instead, they grumbled. They grumbled because they wanted physical provision. They wanted salvation in their own way. They were blinded to how much better what Jesus offered was than what they had asked for. They asked for a piece of bread, and He wanted to give them eternal life. Their answer was to question His authority by asking, "Is not this Jesus the son of Joseph, whose father and mother we know?" (John 6:42). Jesus unabashedly declared to be the Son of God. He proclaimed the Father's sovereign hand in salvation. This salvation was not dependent on man's ability to earn it but on God's ability. All the Father draws will come, and all who come to Jesus in faith will be saved.

"I am the bread of life." This is the first of seven "I Am" statements by Jesus. These statements declare who Jesus is and identify Jesus as Yahweh. He is the promised Messiah and the One history had been longing for. The manna of the book of Exodus was but a picture that pointed to Jesus who was the true manna. Jesus calls all to come, to eat and drink. This is a call to believe—believe in the One who was the plan from before time began, to believe and live, to believe and be satisfied forever.

We are not unlike those who wanted physical provision instead of the good and better gift that Jesus offered. This passage calls us to hunger and thirst for Jesus more than we hunger and thirst for the temporary provision of the world. We are called to feast on what matters for eternity. We are called to believe in Jesus, to trust in Jesus, and to rest in Jesus. This passage should fill the hearts of every believer with confidence and hope. Our salvation is not dependent on us but on God. As Paul told us in Romans 8:35-39, there is nothing that can separate us from the love of God. So, we rest not in our ability to hold fast to Jesus but in the truth that He is holding fast to us. We will fail, but He never will. God will keep us, sustain us, and satisfy us. Fullness and joy are found only in Him.

DAY 2 QUESTIONS

1. IN WHAT WAYS ARE YOU SOMETIMES TEMPTED TO SEEK PHYSICAL PROVISION THAT LASTS FOR A MOMENT INSTEAD OF ETERNAL PROVISION?

2. READ EXODUS 16. HOW DOES THIS PASSAGE HELP YOU UNDERSTAND WHAT IT MEANS THAT JESUS IS THE BREAD OF LIFE?

3. WHAT DOES TODAY'S READING TEACH US ABOUT JESUS? HOW DOES IT GIVE HOPE TO OUR EVERYDAY LIVES?

WEEK 4 DAY 3

"

THIS STORY WOULD BE
A SCANDAL. IT WOULD BE
A SCANDAL OF GRACE.

WORDS OF ETERNAL LIFE

READ: JOHN 6:60-71

It began to become clear to those following Jesus that being a disciple was costly. A follower of Jesus would not just watch while Jesus performed miracles and take part in the miraculous provision of bread. A disciple would be called to lay down his life and choose the bread of life over everything that the world had to offer. There were many who had chosen to follow Jesus because they thought it would bring good things in life, but Jesus was slowly revealing that the path of following Him would involve laying down everything else.

Jesus was showing that water being turned into wine was more about the transformation of hearts than wine at a wedding and that feeding thousands had more to do with the provision that only God can give than a free dinner. People were being called to believe, lay down their lives, and trust this man from Galilee. At the realization of what true discipleship is, many walked away. Jesus asked those following Him if they would walk away too. Was it too much to follow Jesus? Was it too costly, too heavy, and too hard? A firm but gentle reminder came from His lips, reminding them that they never could do it on their own. Following Him and believing in Him were hard things that were made possible only because of the grace of the Father.

Being a follower of Jesus is always worth it.

The passage tells us that many turned away on that day. Perhaps they had been uneasy and wondering what they had gotten themselves into. When given the option to walk away, they jumped at the opportunity. As the crowds scattered due to the cost of discipleship, Jesus asked the same questions of the twelve: "You don't want to go away too, do you?" Simon Peter stepped forward for the twelve with some of the most moving words in all of Scripture: "Lord, to whom will we go?" Peter's question and the words that followed did not deny that being a disciple is often difficult, because it is. The words did not paint a picture of prosperity or a life of ease for God's children. Instead, Peter's words rang out through the silence, that being a follower of Jesus is always worth it. What other comfort is there for the hurting? What water can quench the thirsty soul? What provision will endure forever? Only Jesus. Life is found in Him alone.

Even while the words were spoken, there was one in their midst who did not agree. Judas would soon choose the fleeting pleasures of a few silver coins over the constant comfort of a Savior. Jesus was not fooled by outward affirmations or the guise of religiosity. Jesus knows the heart. He knew that He would be betrayed by one of His own. This story would be a scandal. It would be a scandal of grace.

The sentiments of this passage are not foreign to our own culture. There are many who want to claim the name of Jesus without following His commands. There are many who speak in jest of their devotion to Jesus. With phrases like, "I love Jesus…but…" they prove that their love is not true. They would rather have the temporary pleasures of the world than count the cost of following Jesus. May this not be true of us.

Being a disciple is not a guarantee of wealth or a life of ease. It is not a guarantee that life will be problem free. In fact, the life of a disciple is often one of suffering as we follow in the footsteps of our Savior. But the promise of the gospel is that we will never be alone. The promise of the gospel is that even our worst days are being used to transform us. The promise of the gospel is that there is a day when sorrow and suffering will be forever gone and that all of the pain of this life will have been worth it because of the surpassing worth of Jesus.

So Peter's words call us to make a decision to be all in for Jesus. Resting in the Father's sovereign grace, we can declare that we have decided to follow Jesus. We will not turn back, not because of some supposed goodness in ourselves but because of the steadfast love and grace of our God who has drawn us to Himself and who will sustain us until we breath our final breath. And when the day comes and we awake in God's presence, we will know that following Jesus is worth it. The God who saved us by His grace will sustain us by His grace.

DAY 3 QUESTIONS

1 WHAT IS THE COST OF FOLLOWING JESUS?

2 WHAT IS THE BLESSING OF FOLLOWING JESUS?

3 HOW DOES THIS PASSAGE ENCOURAGE YOU TO TRUST THE LORD EVEN WHEN LIFE IS DIFFICULT?

WEEK 4 DAY 4

"

WHO IS JESUS? THAT IS THE QUESTION THAT EVERY PERSON MUST ANSWER.

WHO IS JESUS?

READ: JOHN 7:1-36

CROSS REFERENCE:

Isaiah 53:10

Psalm 31:14-15

Chapter 7 picks up several months later in Jesus's ministry at the time of the Feast of Booths or Feast of Tabernacles. This chapter overflows with twenty questions. Jesus's ministry was leaving those He encountered curious about who He was and what exactly He had come to do. Who is Jesus? That is a question that every person must answer. If Jesus is who He says that He is, then this demands a response in the hearts and lives of every person.

The Feast of Booths was one of the most joyful times of year for the people of Israel. This feast was a celebration of God's faithfulness to lead the people through the wilderness when then they lived in tents (tabernacles or booths). It was also a celebration of God sending the rain and the harvest for the year. It was a time of celebration and rejoicing over the faithfulness and provision of God. As the feast drew near, the religious leaders were rising up against Jesus. They wanted to kill Him. Jesus's own brothers did not believe who He was, and their words to Him seem almost like a dare to go declare who He is at the feast. Jesus answered them simply that His time had not come.

His presence shone light on the darkness of their sin.

Jesus described the world as hating Him because He revealed their sin. He was the Light of the world and His presence shone light on the darkness of their sin. The Jews spoke of Him at the feast, and the people sought to answer the question of who Jesus was. Some thought that He was a good man, and others thought that He was deceiving the people, a serious charge under the law of Moses. The religious leaders of the day sought to reveal the sin of others and then shamed them for it, but Jesus was different. Jesus revealed the sin of the people and came to remove their shame. Jesus was not like other religious leaders. He spoke with authority, and the people were amazed at how He spoke. Yet, they questioned His credentials. Where did He get the authority to teach the way that He did? Jesus's answer was that the authority He spoke with was from the One who had sent Him.

The response of the people stands in sharp contrast to the response of Peter in chapter 6. Peter had humbly recognized Jesus as the Messiah and the One with the words of eternal life. The people questioned, doubted, and even accused Jesus. Could this Jesus actually be the Messiah? Could He actually be speaking with authority from God? Jesus was not at all what the religious leaders expected in their Messiah. They were looking for someone to overthrow governments, but instead, Jesus was overthrowing their religious system. They were expecting someone to return glory to Israel, but instead Jesus was revealing that He Himself was the true glory of Israel. To those who looked on, Jesus was nothing more than a carpenter's son. But Jesus was the Son of God, who had come to set the captives free.

They wanted to arrest Him. His teaching was too radical. But verse 30 tells us that they did not even lay their hands on Him because His hour had not come. These words should plant our hope firmly in the sovereignty of God. God is in control. His plan would be accomplished. Those men who sought to arrest Him could not even touch Jesus without the permission of the Father. They were powerless to carry out their plans until the Lord allowed it. Their hands were tied, and they could not have arrested Him if they had tried. Jesus still had work to do. People were believing in Him despite the anger of the religious leaders. There would be a moment when evil men would arrest Him, beat Him, and kill Him. But it would not happen yet. And when it happened it would be the Father's plan. Isaiah 53:10 tells us that it was the Father's will to crush Him. This was the plan. This was always the plan. The Holy One would come as a sacrifice to redeem a people for God. God's plan was a plan of redemption.

We can find hope and encouragement in these verses. We can rest in God's sovereign grace and tender care for His children. God's plan will come to pass. All wrongs will be made right in God's time. If we are waiting, it is because God has determined that it is good for us to wait. If we are suffering, we can rest in knowing that nothing can take place without His permission. He is using even our sufferings and our waiting in His plan. We look to Jesus who has walked before us as our example. We look to Jesus, and we trust that God is using every season of waiting and every sorrow of suffering to make us like Him. We rest in the promise of Psalm 31:14-15, that our times are in His hands. We trust Him when we do not understand. We trust Him when we cannot see what He is doing. We trust Him when the wait is long. Trusting Him does not mean that we understand; it means we trust Him even when we do not understand.

Who is Jesus? He is everything.

DAY 4 QUESTIONS

1   IF YOU WERE ASKED, WHO IS JESUS IS, WHAT WOULD YOUR ANSWER BE?

2   HOW DOES JESUS EXPOSE OUR SIN?

3   WHAT DOES THIS PASSAGE TEACH US ABOUT GOD'S TIMING AND GOD'S PLAN?

WEEK 4   DAY 5

"

WITHOUT THE GRACE OF GOD, WE DO NOT EVEN KNOW THAT WE ARE THIRSTY.

LIVING WATER

READ: JOHN 7:37-52

CROSS REFERENCE:

Isaiah 12:3

Isaiah 55:1

It was during the Feast of Booths that the people had asked questions of who Jesus was. Now, at the end of the feast, we see Jesus make an impassioned plea to the pilgrims before they departed for their homes. His plea was an offer of living water. It was an offer of Himself.

The final scene of chapter 7 is a striking one. It was the last day of this joyous feast. Water rituals had just taken place to remember the Exodus and God's provision of water in the desert, to praise God for the harvest and the rain that made it possible, and to look forward to the day when the Messiah would come and bring the water of salvation (Isaiah 12:3). In the midst of this joyful hope and expectation, Jesus stood to His feet with a message for all. In the midst of a celebration thanking God for the waters of provision and looking forward in hope to the day that the Messiah would come, Jesus declared to be the promised water of salvation about which Isaiah had prophesied.

Jesus is the water that our parched souls crave.

The image of water and thirst is one seen throughout Scripture. It is a poignant picture which every person can relate. Without water, we are dead. It is easy for us to take this truth for granted if we live in a western context where clean drinking water is readily accessible. But these first century Jews would have had a deeper picture of the desperate need for water in their dry, desert climate. Specifically, during this celebration, they would have also been familiar with their ancestors' need for water to be provided in the desert to sustain the children of Israel while they wandered in the wilderness. Jesus was offering something necessary and precious.

Thirst is one of our most important senses. Thirst tells us that we are missing something that we desperately need. This is true of our physical thirst for water and also of the spiritual thirst that is given to us by a gracious God. Without the grace of God, we do not even know that we are thirsty. Without His kindness and mercy, we do not even know that we need Him.

Jesus was offering a priceless treasure. He was offering Himself. He was the promised Messiah for whom they had waited. He was the living water that they craved. His call was for them to come and to drink. He offered water without a cost (Isaiah 55:1). This water was not something that could be earned. It was not something that could be worked for. It was a gift offered freely to all who would believe. Here again we see the key theme of belief that is throughout the entire book of John. Jesus came so that men and women, young and old, rich and poor might believe. He came to bring water that would forever satisfy. He promised rivers of living water, not just a sip or a cup, but overflowing and abundant water. Jesus is the source of this provision, and He is the provision itself. He is the gift and the giver.

Jesus spoke with compassion and authority, and it left some of the people shaken up. Who Jesus is demands a response. Some ran to Him in worship, others doubted and were unsure, and even others conspired to arrest Him. But His time had not come, and they were powerless to touch Him until the moment that God allowed. Yet it was clear—there had never been a man like this man. This man who came offering water for the thirsty and bread to the hungry was unlike any other man.

Jesus is the water that our parched souls crave. Our thirst for Him is a gift from Him. It tells us that we need Him and points us to the only One who satisfies. He tells us that we need Him, and then He gives us Himself. He does not leave us thirsting a moment too long. He offers the water, and He provides it from the abundance of His love. He comes bringing grace and hope because He comes bringing Himself. The water of His grace is not just for the moment of our salvation but for every moment of our lives. The gospel is for every day. The gospel changes everything. His grace is new every morning, and each day He calls us to come, drink, and find our souls satisfied in Him alone.

DAY 5 QUESTIONS

1. WHY DO YOU THINK THE CROWDS WERE GETTING CONCERNED OVER JESUS' TEACHING AT THIS POINT?

2. THE PICTURE OF WATER AND THIRST IS SEEN THROUGHOUT SCRIPTURE. LOOK UP THE FOLLOWING PASSAGES, AND RECORD HOW THEY HELP YOU UNDERSTAND THIS POWERFUL SYMBOL:

    ISAIAH 12:3

    ISAIAH 55:1

    REVELATION 21:6

    REVELATION 22:17

    PSALM 63:1-8

3. HOW DOES JESUS SATISFY OUR SOULS?

WEEK 4

SCRIPTURE MEMORY

JOHN 1:6-7

There was a man sent from God whose name was John. He came as a witness to testify about the light, so that all might believe through him.

WEEK FOUR REFLECTION

REVIEW
John 6:1 – 7:52

PARAPHRASE THE PASSAGE FROM THIS WEEK.

WHAT DID YOU OBSERVE FROM THIS WEEK'S TEXT ABOUT GOD AND HIS CHARACTER?

WHAT DOES THIS WEEK'S PASSAGE REVEAL ABOUT THE CONDITION OF MANKIND AND YOURSELF?

HOW DOES THIS PASSAGE POINT TO THE GOSPEL?

HOW SHOULD YOU RESPOND TO THIS PASSAGE? WHAT SPECIFIC ACTION STEPS CAN YOU TAKE THIS WEEK TO APPLY THIS PASSAGE?

WRITE A PRAYER OF RESPONSE TO YOUR STUDY OF GOD'S WORD.

Adore God for who He is, confess sins that He revealed in your own life, ask Him to empower you to walk in obedience, and pray for anyone who comes to mind as you study.

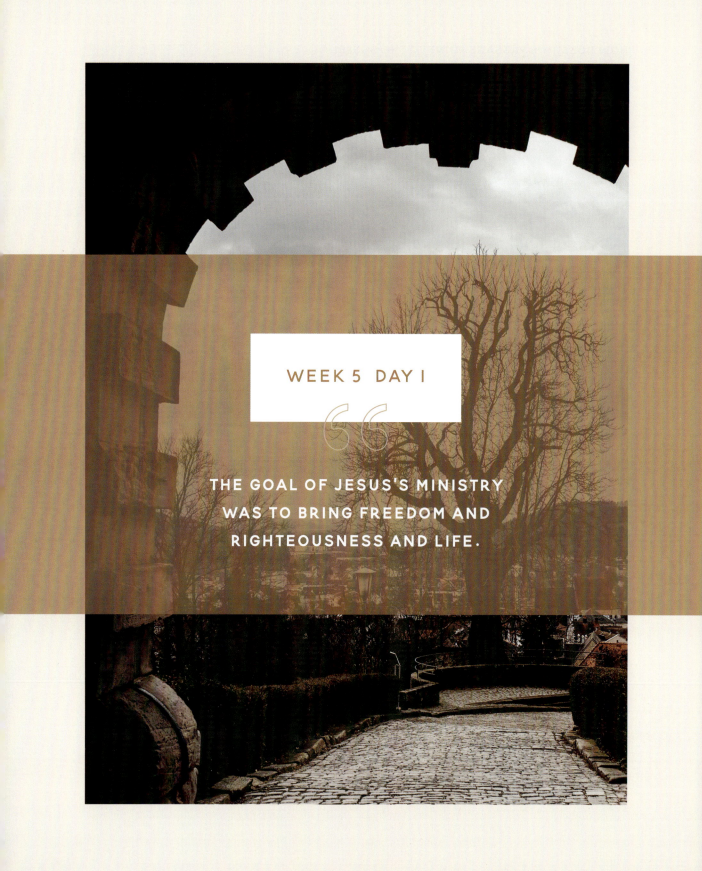

WEEK 5 DAY 1

> THE GOAL OF JESUS'S MINISTRY WAS TO BRING FREEDOM AND RIGHTEOUSNESS AND LIFE.

FOR US

READ: JOHN 7:53-8:11

CROSS REFERENCE:

2 Peter 1:21

Romans 8

As we come to this passage of Scripture, you may notice that your Bible includes something like: "[The earliest manuscripts do not include 7:53-8:11]." This may have raised questions in your mind about the reliability of the text at hand. Before we address what this note means, let us start by affirming what we believe about Scripture. We believe that the Bible is inerrant. When we say that the Bible is inerrant, we are stating that the Bible is completely true in all it affirms, and there are no mistakes or errors. And we believe, as we just read, that the Bible was written by God through men—men spoke from God as they were carried along by the Holy Spirit (2 Peter 1:21). These men were moved by the Holy Spirit—carried along by Him—to write down God's Word in original writings, and then these writings were copied and preserved and passed down to us.

The most famous Greek New Testament, the one used to write the King James version, relied upon Greek manuscripts from the 12th and 13th centuries. These were all from one particular family of texts, which were themselves late. Since then, a number of

> ## Even as Jesus is for the adulteress woman, we have God who is relentlessly for us.

earlier manuscripts have been found, which scholars believe more reliably represent what the original words of the New Testament were. The earlier in the process, the less chance for mistakes to creep in. It is the same thing here. The general principle is that earlier (closer to the original) is better.

This particular passage of Scripture is not found in those earliest manuscripts, and that is why most of our translations today include that statement in brackets. With that said, there are two things we can take away. First of all, even if this story is not original, it could represent a real event in Jesus's life. Perhaps we are drawn to this story because in it, we see Jesus putting the scribes and Pharisees in their place and showing mercy and grace to a woman accused of sin. It has the ring of truth. This was likely a story that was passed around orally and eventually was written down and placed into the book of John.

Even still, this is a beautiful story, and within the story, there is an incredible truth found all throughout the Bible. The Pharisees and scribes bring forth a woman who was caught in adultery. They are trying to trap Jesus. Either He will pardon the woman and they will accuse Him of rejecting the law of Moses or He will agree that she should be killed and do something Roman law did not give them the right to do. But here we see Jesus stoop down and write something in the sand. They are persistent in their questions. And Jesus then stands up and declares, "The one without sin among you should be the first to throw a stone at her." The Pharisees' wicked hearts are exposed, and they walk away one by one. Once Jesus is left alone with the women, He asks her, "Woman, where are they? Has no one condemned you?" She replies, "No one, Lord." And then we hear the Lord's sweet words full of mercy and grace, "Neither do I condemn you… Go, and from now on do not sin anymore."

What a beautiful picture of grace and truth! He is merciful to her to release her without judgment and then gives her a challenge to flee sin and live in holiness. He does not condemn her, and nothing was required from her to merit His pardon. He has extended mercy and grace to her because of His very nature. This is exactly what He does for us—He extends grace, mercy, and love before we have even made the first step toward Him. This is the grace of the gospel, and this is the same grace of the gospel we see in Romans 8.

The goal of Jesus's ministry was to bring freedom and righteousness and life. He did not come to condemn the world but to save it. The same offer that He gave to the adulteress woman is the same offer extended to us in the redeeming hope of the gospel. If we turn from our sins and believe in Jesus's death and resurrection—trusting in Him as our mediator with God—Jesus becomes the fulfillment of the law's requirement that we be holy. Instead of condemnation, we know only acceptance before God—not on the basis of our performance but as a permanent position. And once we are accepted by God, it does not matter who wants to throw rocks at us.

Even as Jesus is for the adulteress woman, we have God who is relentlessly for us. What will He not give if He already gave us the costliest gift of all—the gift of His own dear Son? If God has declared us right with Him—who can declare us wrong, whether friends or enemies or our own fearful hearts? And through it all, Jesus—the very One who paid our debt and became condemned in our place—He is the One, now raised in victorious life, who speaks for us—reminding the Father that He has paid for all our sins and forever insuring that the condemnation will never come back.

In response to His boundless mercy, let us go and sin no more for the glory of His great name and in a way that displays the shocking mercy and boundless grace of our loving Lord.

DAY 1 QUESTIONS

1. WHAT DOES THIS PASSAGE TEACH US ABOUT WHO JESUS IS?

2. READ ROMANS 8:1. HOW DOES THIS VERSE, ALONG WITH TODAY'S PASSAGE, HELP YOU UNDERSTAND WHAT IT MEANS FOR THERE TO BE NO CONDEMNATION FOR GOD'S PEOPLE.

3. WHAT SHOULD YOUR RESPONSE BE TO HIS BOUNDLESS MERCY IN YOUR OWN LIFE?

WEEK 5 DAY 2

"

THE LIGHT OF THE WORLD
IS WHO WE WERE MADE TO LONG FOR.

LIGHT OF THE WORLD

READ: JOHN 8:12-30

CROSS REFERENCE:

Exodus 13:21

Exodus 14:19-20

Isaiah 42:6

Isaiah 49:6

Psalm 27:1

Revelation 21:22-27

The "I Am" statements of Jesus are some of the most significant statements in helping us to understand the message of this gospel. These statements declare who Jesus is and call for belief in Him alone. It is in this passage that we see the second of the "I Am" statements in the book of John.

These statements again take place in the context of the Feast of Booths and the celebration of God's deliverance of the people of Israel from slavery and through the wilderness wanderings. At this crucial time of year when the people of Israel looked back to the exodus, which was one of their most significant moments in history, Jesus was showing them the truth and the promise of a greater exodus. He was showing them that the exodus itself was meant to point to Him. Jesus had already shown how He was the Bread of Life to which the manna in the wilderness had pointed. He had declared that He was the living water and the provision for their souls, just as God had provided water in the desert for the parched travelers. Now, Jesus tells them that He is the Light of the world.

> These statements declare who Jesus is and call for a belief in Him alone.

Light was an integral part of the celebration in Israel during the Feast of Booths. It celebrated how God had led His children through the wilderness in a pillar of fire and a pillar of cloud (Exodus 13:21, 14:19-20). With the pillars of the temple illuminated during the feast, Jesus declared that He was the Light of the world. The people would have known immediately what He was declaring Himself to be. Aside from the obvious reference to the Exodus, Scripture was overflowing with passages that spoke of the Messiah as the light of the nations (Isaiah 42:6, 49:6). The Psalms also pointed out that God Himself was the light (Psalm 27:1). With the powerful "I Am" phrase echoing God's covenant name, the people knew that Jesus was making a shocking statement about His identity. He was the Messiah the prophets had foretold, and He was God Himself in the flesh.

In the book of Exodus, God's presence was seen as a pillar of fire; it was a shining light that led the people of God. When Jesus declared that He was the Light of the world, He was also giving a command. He was light, and this was a call to follow Him. This was a call to believe. It was a call to go from darkness to light. It should not be surprising to us that the religious leaders wanted none of it. They preferred the darkness of man-made religion to the light of life in God's presence. The light was exposing their sin, and they were content to hide in the darkness.

The religious leaders spewed accusations at Him. In Jewish law, a man could not testify for himself, and that is what they thought that He was doing. So, they accused Him. They did not understand that His word carried much greater weight than any other and that the Father Himself was testifying of the Son. His words infuriated them, but again we are told that His hour had not yet come, so He was not arrested. Jesus warned them that He would go away soon. His words left them confused. The promised Messiah stood in front of them, but they had missed it. Their blinded eyes did not see the light that stood in front of them. He would soon be lifted up on a cross, but the hour had not yet come. Though many of the religious leaders scoffed at Him, the text tells us that many believed. This man who was water, and bread, and light, and life was transforming hearts everywhere He went.

Jesus is the Light of the world. He is the hope of all the earth. Who He is demands a response. We are called to follow Him—to lay down our own plans and our own ways. We are called to walk in the light and flee from the darkness. Following Jesus has a cost. It will call us to turn from the darkness in which we once walked, and to follow Him wherever He leads. But the promise that we cling to as the children of God is that we do not walk alone. Just as God led the children of Israel with a pillar of fire, He leads us with the Holy Spirit within us and the Word of God that He has given to us. He calls us to follow, and then He walks with us every step of the way. He calls us to lay down our lives and then gives us a life of abundance. He calls us to believe. This call is one that happens at the time of our conversion when we place faith in God's saving grace, but it is also a belief that is demonstrated each day as we choose to believe Him for every moment. The Christian life is a life of following. Jesus calls us to follow, and then He leads us.

The final chapters of Revelation end with a description of the new heaven and new earth. Revelation 21:22-27 declares that on that day, there will be no sun or moon because God Himself will be our light. The Light of the world is who we were made to long for, and someday the light of our God will be the only light that there is, and we will know that all light was meant to point us to the light.

DAY 2 QUESTIONS

1. READ EXODUS 13:21, 14:19-20; ISAIAH 42:6, 49:6; PSALM 27:1; REVELATION 21:22-27. HOW DOES THIS PICTURE OF LIGHT HELP YOU UNDERSTAND MORE OF WHO JESUS IS?

2. THROUGHOUT THE LAST CHAPTERS, THIS CONCEPT OF JESUS' HOUR NOT HAVING COME YET IS SEEN. WHAT DOES THIS TEACH YOU ABOUT GOD'S SOVEREIGNTY? HOW DOES THAT MAKE YOU THINK DIFFERENTLY ABOUT YOUR OWN LIFE?

3. IN WHAT AREA OF YOUR LIFE IS GOD CALLING YOU TO TRUST HIM RIGHT NOW? IN WHAT AREA IS HE CALLING YOU TO FOLLOW?

WEEK 5 DAY 3

"

JESUS CAME TO SEEK THE HEARTS
OF MEN AND WOMEN.

SET FREE

READ: JOHN 8:31-38

Jesus is our freedom. He is our source of life. As Jesus spoke to the crowds with the religious leaders looking on, He spoke of the life and freedom that are found in being true disciples. Throughout the book of John thus far, we have seen many believing on the Lord. But all who said that they believed were not true disciples. Some claimed to believe, simply because they had seen miracles. The wonder of bread and wine had drawn their attention, but they had not truly placed their faith in Jesus. In this passage, Jesus speaks to those who were following Him and tells them what it means to be a true disciple.

Jesus came to seek the hearts of men and women. He came to bring them into the family of God. He wanted them to understand the cost of discipleship. He called the disciples to leave everything to follow Him, and now He speaks to the crowd in a similar way. He tells them that those who are truly His disciples will abide in His Word. To abide means "to dwell, remain, or hold fast." Jesus will later liken this concept to a branch that is clinging to the vine. As followers of Jesus, we cling to Him who is the source of our life. Our nourishment flows from Him, our hope flows from Him, and our lives flow from Him. We cling to His word. For the people in Jesus's day, they were literally hanging on His every Word. For us today, we are clinging to His Word revealed in Scripture.

> Jesus is our freedom.
> He is our source of life.

We know truth through the Word. The truth sets us free from sin and from legalism. It sets us free from our tendency to rebel against God and His goodness, and it sets us free from our inclination to legalistic rules and regulations. For the rebel and the religious, freedom is found in Jesus. In Him alone is freedom from the sin that holds us captive. In Him alone is freedom from the oppression of man-made religious systems that tell us to work our way to God. Jesus came to offer a better way. He came to offer Himself.

Jesus spoke of the freedom that is found in the truth, and the religious people listening in were not sure what to think. They responded to Him with their credentials. They were children of Abraham. In today's language, they were telling Him that they had grown up in a religious family, they had been moral people, and they had come to the worship services. As children of Abraham they claimed to be free people. Certainly, they were not enslaved. They were missing the point. They were slaves to their sin, and they did not even know that they were held captive. Their chains were so tight that they could not even feel them.

Jesus came offering freedom, and the freedom He brings is a forever freedom. Through faith in His grace, we become the sons and daughters of God. In Him, we have found a forever family. Because of Jesus, our chains are broken. True freedom is found only in Jesus. This world will try to offer a picture of freedom in which you can do whatever you want and no one will try to stop you. But the gospel offers freedom that penetrates to every part of your soul. It is a freedom that sets you free from the weight of your sin and free from trying to earn salvation. Instead, this freedom unites your heart in relationship with Christ and changes your heart to desire to bring Him glory. Freedom is a gift. Grace is a gift. And Jesus is the source of these good gifts.

As disciples of Jesus today, the command to abide in His Word is for us as well. We know the truth that sets us free through the living and abiding Word of God. It may be tempting for us to think that obedience would have been easier for those in the accounts we are reading. We think it would have been better if we could have seen Jesus face to face and heard these words come from His lips. But we have something that those listening in that day did not have. We have God's written Word, and we have the Spirit inside us to guide us into all truth. We are called to abide in Him, and the way that we do that is through His Word. We must run to His Word because this is where freedom is found. The gospel sets us free. His grace sets us free.

Now the call for the people of God is for us to abide in Him and in His Word. We draw life from God's Word like a branch draws life from the vine. We persevere, not because we are holding on to Him but because He is holding on to us. He has grafted us in, and He will not let us go. We are His forever. May we forever praise His matchless name.

DAY 3 QUESTIONS

1   HOW CAN YOU PRACTICALLY ABIDE IN GOD'S WORD?

2   WHAT ARE SOME THINGS THAT ENSLAVE PEOPLE?

3   WHAT DOES IT MEAN TO BE FREE? HOW ARE WE FREE IN CHRIST?

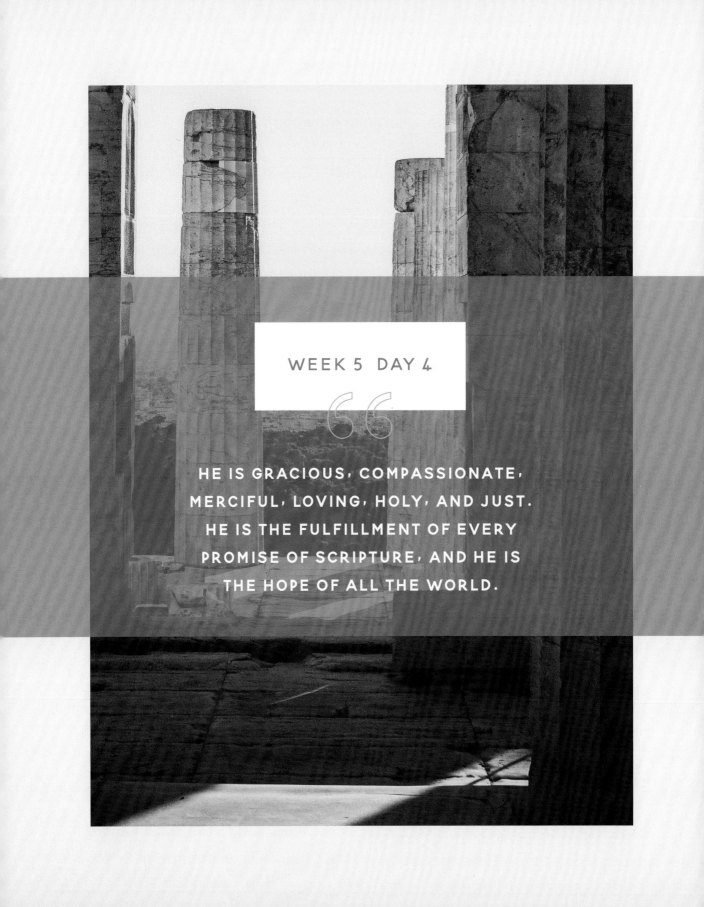

WEEK 5 DAY 4

"

HE IS GRACIOUS, COMPASSIONATE, MERCIFUL, LOVING, HOLY, AND JUST. HE IS THE FULFILLMENT OF EVERY PROMISE OF SCRIPTURE, AND HE IS THE HOPE OF ALL THE WORLD.

I AM

READ: JOHN 8:39-59

The response of the people to Jesus was confusion and accusation. They claimed Abraham as their father, but Jesus pointed out that they did not act or live like Abraham. Jesus confronts their unbelief. They were not sons of Abraham or sons of God. His words would have left them shocked. But Jesus went even a step further when He told them that their father was the devil. They were believing lies and rejecting the way, the truth, and the life that stood in front of them.

The Jews answered back with more accusations as they stood wondering who this man was who had spoken such strong warnings to them. They accused Him of being a Samaritan, and they accused Him of having a demon. Jesus denied these accusations, and then made a statement even more striking than those He had already made. He told them that those who kept His word would never see death. The statement seemed utterly preposterous to them. They pointed again to Abraham who was the father of the Jewish religion and the one who the nation looked to as its founder. Even Abraham had died, so was Jesus better than these

They were blinded to the promises of God and the One who stood in front of them.

patriarchs and prophets that they revered so greatly? Still Jesus persisted that God the Father had sent Him and was glorifying Him. He was showing them their own weakness. Jesus revealed to them their desperate need and stood with open arms as the solution to their need.

Jesus made a statement in verse 56 that Abraham rejoiced to see the day of Jesus; he saw it and was glad. This verse is a reminder to us of the one way of salvation that is the theme of the Old and New Testaments. This theme is Jesus Himself. From Abraham to the prophets, to the moment that Jesus spoke these words, and to today, the way of salvation has been through Jesus. Abraham, in faith, looked forward to the promised Messiah and placed faith in Jesus. The text tells us that Abraham saw it and was glad. Though scholars have discussed how exactly Abraham saw, we can point to the fulfilled promises of God that were made to Abraham. Abraham was promised a son, and that son would be a picture of a greater Son of Israel who was yet to come. Abraham saw that God keeps His promises in the birth of the miracle son, Isaac. And if He kept His promise of a son, He would also keep His promise of a deliverer who would come through Abraham's line. This son of Abraham was Jesus Himself who had come to offer hope and salvation to the lost and the weary.

Still the people scoffed at the claims He made. He was not old enough to have lived to see Abraham generations ago. They were blinded to the promises of God and the One who stood in front of them. This man was the Son of God, the promised Messiah, and the Savior of Abraham. Jesus's replied to their persistent questions was one final statement: "Truly I tell you, before Abraham was, I am." This statement carried more significance. In it, He evoked the covenant name of God. God had revealed Himself to Moses as "I AM," and now Jesus was laying claim to that title. He was declaring Himself to be eternal, and He was declaring Himself to be the covenant God. Jesus is the "I AM." He was their Creator. He was God made flesh. Their response should have been to bow before Him in worship, but instead they picked up stones to kill Him. His time had not yet come, so He would not be harmed, but their hatred for Him was growing. This man of love and grace was hated by many of the people to whom He had come to offer salvation.

Jesus was maligned and hated. The people did not understand Him or the way that He lived. They threatened and accused Him. As followers of Jesus, we must know that as the world hated Him, so it will hate us. The people's hearts were hardened by their sin. They claimed to be the children of God, but they did not know Him. They claimed to follow God, and yet as He stood in front of them, they did not recognize Him. God Himself spoke to them, and they did not recognize His voice. Their hatred did not change who He is. He is gracious, compassionate, merciful, loving, holy, and just. He is the fulfillment of every promise of Scripture, and He is the hope of all the world. May we be men and women who believe. May we be people who recognize His voice and answer His call to follow. May we serve Him joyfully in a world that may not understand. May we rest in Jesus and Jesus alone.

DAY 4 QUESTIONS

1 WHY WERE JESUS' CLAIMS SO OFFENSIVE TO THE PEOPLE?

2 WHAT DO WE LEARN ABOUT JESUS FROM THIS PASSAGE?

3 WHY IS IT IMPORTANT WE UNDERSTAND THAT ALL OF THE BIBLE POINTS TO JESUS?

WEEK 5 DAY 5

> THE LIGHT OF THE WORLD BREAKS THROUGH
> THE DARKNESS OF OUR BLINDNESS.
> THIS IS WHY JESUS CAME.

I ONCE WAS BLIND, BUT NOW I SEE

READ: JOHN 9:1-41

CROSS REFERENCE:

Psalm 146:7-8
Isaiah 29:18
Isaiah 35:5
Isaiah 42:7

Chapter 9 centers on one event in the life of Jesus. It is here that we see Jesus give sight to a man born blind. In this miracle, we see one of the greatest demonstrations of what the gospel does and what salvation is. Through Christ, the blind can see. Perhaps this is why the restoration of sight to the blind is the most frequent type of miracle throughout the gospel accounts. And perhaps this is why John Newton penned the words: "Amazing grace how sweet the sound that saved a wreth like me! I once was lost, but now am found. Was blind, but now I see," in perhaps the most famous hymn of all time. There seems to be no better illustration that Jesus could have given to show that He is the Light of the world than to let a man who had seen only darkness for his entire life see the light.

We serve a God who gives sight to those blinded by their sin.

The passage begins with a question from the disciples about the reason that this man had been born blind. But this question leads us to a broader question of human suffering. Why do people suffer? The disciples immediately assumed that this suffering must be the result of sin. And while some suffering is the result of our sin, Jesus makes it clear that that is not always the case. Ultimately suffering exists for the glory of God. That may seem like a perplexing statement at first glance. But understanding this truth can transform the way we think about suffering in our own lives and in the lives of those with whom we interact.

Jesus healed the man in an instant, and in that moment, everything changed. The man who had been blind all of his life could now see. You would think that the response to this healing would be rejoicing, but the religious leaders met this healing with skepticism. The questions being asked were about the identity of Jesus. Again, the question, "Who is Jesus?" is underlying so many of the events that we see take place in the book of John. Was He a good man like many believed? Or a kind teacher? Was He possessed by a demon like some had accused? Or was He something so much more? When questioned, the healed man was not sure how to answer. Yet he proclaimed that he had once been blind, but now he could see. In an instant, everything had been made new.

The physical conversion that this man experienced paled in comparison to the spiritual conversion that took place at the end of the chapter. Jesus reveals Himself as the promised Son of Man, and the man believes and worships the One who had healed not only his body but his soul.

The final verses of the chapter show the great problem of the Pharisees. These religious leaders claimed to see just fine, but Jesus identified them as blind men. They scoffed at the thought. The words of Jesus confirm the words of John's prologue. Jesus had come as the light, but many would reject Him and prefer the darkness of blindness to the light of His grace. They were blind to the undeniable fact that they were indeed blind. Stuck in their pride, they were blinded to the Light of the world who stood before them.

We serve a God who gives sight to those blinded by their sin. This truth is one that is found throughout Scripture. Psalm 146:7-8 describes the Lord as one who sets prisoners free and opens the eyes of the blind. The book of Isaiah repeats this refrain over and over. The Messiah was coming to open the eyes that were once blind (Isaiah 29:18, 35:5, 42:7). The Light of the world breaks through the darkness of our blindness. This is why Jesus came.

Believers who read these words can rejoice that their blindness has been replaced with sight. These words should also stir our hearts to pray for friends, loved ones, and those who we have never met who are still blinded by their sin. We can pray God will open their blinded eyes to the light of His goodness and grace. This passage should also encourage us in our suffering, whatever it may be. We can rest in hope that any suffering that we face in this world that is broken by sin and the fall is for the ultimate purpose of God's glory. Sometimes the glory of God is revealed in how He delivers us from our suffering, and other times His glory is revealed by giving His children the strength to endure. The truth is that we may not ever know exactly why we were called to suffer in a specific way, but we can rest our hope in the One who has made our blinded eyes to see.

DAY 5 QUESTIONS

1 HOW IS THIS MIRACLE A PICTURE OF SALVATION?

2 WHAT DOES THIS PASSAGE TEACH US ABOUT SUFFERING?

3 WHAT DO WE LEARN ABOUT JESUS FROM THIS PASSAGE?

WEEK 5

SCRIPTURE MEMORY

JOHN 1:8-9

He was not the light, but he came to testify about the light. The true light that gives light to everyone, was coming into the world.

WEEK FIVE REFLECTION

REVIEW
John 7:53 – 9:41

PARAPHRASE THE PASSAGE FROM THIS WEEK.

WHAT DID YOU OBSERVE FROM THIS WEEK'S TEXT ABOUT GOD AND HIS CHARACTER?

WHAT DOES THIS WEEK'S PASSAGE REVEAL ABOUT THE CONDITION OF MANKIND AND YOURSELF?

HOW DOES THIS PASSAGE POINT TO THE GOSPEL?

_____
_____
_____
_____
_____
_____
_____

HOW SHOULD YOU RESPOND TO THIS PASSAGE? WHAT SPECIFIC ACTION STEPS CAN YOU TAKE THIS WEEK TO APPLY THIS PASSAGE?

_____
_____
_____
_____
_____
_____
_____

WRITE A PRAYER OF RESPONSE TO YOUR STUDY OF GOD'S WORD.

Adore God for who He is, confess sins that He revealed in your own life, ask Him to empower you to walk in obedience, and pray for anyone who comes to mind as you study.

_____
_____
_____
_____
_____
_____

WEEK 6 DAY 1

❝

JESUS IS A SHEPHERD WHO TENDERLY AND COMPASSIONATELY LOVES HIS PEOPLE.

THEY KNOW HIS VOICE

READ: JOHN 10:1-6

CROSS REFERENCE:

Ezekiel 34
Psalm 23
Psalm 79:13
Psalm 80:1
Isaiah 40:11
John 6:37
Hebrews 4:15

Immediately after the man was healed of his blindness and was cast out by the Pharisees, Jesus begins to speak of the true Shepherd of Israel. The imagery of a shepherd and his sheep was one that would have been commonly understood in the society to which Jesus was speaking. Most families owned sheep, and they commonly understood the role of a shepherd in caring for his sheep. Jesus was also clearly referencing Ezekiel 34 where God condemned the evil shepherds who were the leaders who had failed to lead the people of Israel to the Lord.

The image of God as Shepherd and His people as sheep is not a new concept. It is one that is seen throughout Scripture. Psalm 23 is perhaps the most famous example of God being a shepherd to His own, but the same concept can be seen in other passages like Psalm 79:13, 80:1, and Isaiah 40:11. The nation of Israel's history had been full of judges, kings, prophets, and leaders who had sought to shepherd them. Some of these leaders were faithful men, and others were evil leaders. But with the coming of Jesus, we learn that all of these shepherds were pointing toward and making the people's hearts yearn for the one true Shepherd.

In love, God takes the first step toward the lost and the broken.

The Pharisees were just like the evil shepherds the prophet Ezekiel had warned about. They were selfish men who cared about themselves above all. They had twisted God's holy law to serve their own interests. They had neglected the poor. They looked religious on the outside, but their hearts were far from the Lord.

But Jesus is different.

Jesus is a shepherd who tenderly and compassionately loves His people. He was not a robber and a thief who had sneaked in to the sheepfold. He had come through the door and been sent by the Father to rescue His own. He would defend His sheep from these false shepherds. His sheep had been given to Him by the Father (John 6:37). The sheep came to Him because the Father, in love, had drawn them. In love, God takes the first step toward the lost and the broken. The sheep hear His voice. God's people recognize His calling.

What a sweet promise it is that He calls His sheep by name. In mercy and in grace, He pursues them by name. Shepherds at this time would name their sheep. These names were usually designated by their characteristics such as "short tail" or "spotted ear." Each sheep was unique, and the shepherd knew each of their names, each of their backgrounds, and everything about them. What a stunning picture of redemption that God calls us by name. He knows everything about us, and yet He calls us out to be His own. This is the love of our Good Shepherd.

God's people are then marked by hearing His voice and following Him. The sheep are not left on their own. Jesus goes before them. His people are now called to follow in His steps and walk in the ways that He has walked before us. We can rest in the truth that we serve a high priest who has been tempted in every way that we have been, yet without sin (Hebrews 4:15). He has felt rejection and suffering. He has felt grief and loss. We look to our Shepherd, and we follow Him. This is what we are called to do. In the world, there will be many competing voices, but we listen for the voice of our Shepherd.

The contrast is clear. The Shepherd's own hear and know His voice. But the religious leaders standing there did not understand what He was saying. The allegory that He set before them made no sense to their ears.

As the people of God who have been called out by name, it is now our joy to follow our Shepherd as He goes before us. The path may not always be easy, but we are following our Good Shepherd, and He will walk with us every step of the way.

DAY 1 QUESTIONS

1. READ EZEKIEL 34. HOW DOES THIS PASSAGE HELP YOU UNDERSTAND GOD'S HEART AS A SHEPHERD?

2. HOW DOES A GOOD SHEPHERD TREAT HIS SHEEP? WHAT DO WE LEARN ABOUT JESUS IN THIS PASSAGE?

3. WHAT SHOULD YOUR RESPONSE BE TO THE GOOD SHEPHERD? NAME SOME PRACTICAL STEPS YOU CAN TAKE TO RESPOND TO WHAT YOU HAVE LEARNED.

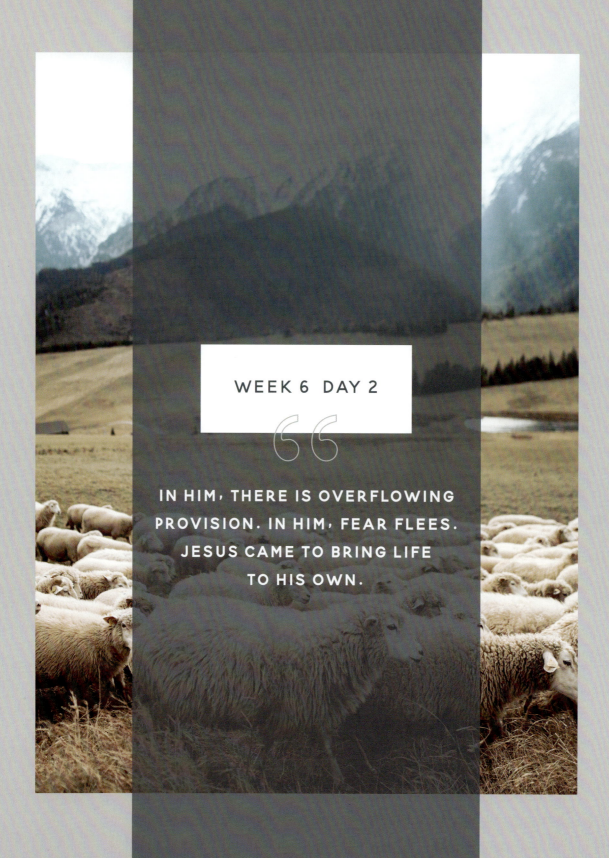

WEEK 6 DAY 2

> IN HIM, THERE IS OVERFLOWING PROVISION. IN HIM, FEAR FLEES. JESUS CAME TO BRING LIFE TO HIS OWN.

THE GOOD SHEPHERD

READ: JOHN 10:7-21

CROSS REFERENCE:

Luke 12:15
Ezekiel 34:11-16
Revelation 7:9-10

The image of a shepherd and sheep is one that is very prominent throughout Scripture. As Jesus continues this discourse, He seeks to deepen the understanding of His listeners to what it means that He is the Good Shepherd. The Old Testament is filled with shepherds, and every one of those shepherds leaves us longing for a better shepherd.

Here, Jesus tells His listeners that He is not only the Good Shepherd but that He is also the door of the sheep. He was showing those who gathered around Him that He is the protector of His own and that He is the only way to life. It has never been popular to say that Jesus is the only way to God, but Jesus boldly declares that He is. There is no other way of salvation. Jesus is the only way.

In Him, the sheep can go in and out and find pasture. He showers them in tender care and protection. His own are safe and protected with Him. In Jesus, the people of God find rest for their souls.

There is no other way of salvation. Jesus is the only way.

In Him there is overflowing provision. In Him, fear flees. Jesus came to bring life to His own. Great emphasis is often placed on the fact that the length of this life is everlasting. But Jesus goes further and focuses on the depth and quality of this life; it is overflowing and abundant. The life that Jesus gives is not just everlasting in its length but also in its depth. It is rich and full because of Jesus Himself. He is good.

Jesus is not teaching a sort of prosperity gospel in any way. In fact, in Luke 12:15 we see Jesus declare that life does not consist in the abundance of possessions. The abundance that He promises is not that of material wealth or a life of ease. This abundance is the abundance of His presence. He is with His children. He is gently leading and guiding like a shepherd guides his sheep. He is calming and comforting. He is ever-present and protects His own. Abundance is found, not because of the gifts that Jesus gives but because Jesus is the greatest gift.

Jesus is careful to point out that there are false shepherds. There are those who sought to lead the people, and yet, they were truly only serving themselves. They were thieves and robbers. They were hired hands who cared more about their own personal gain than they did about the kingdom of God. A hired hand or false shepherd had the initial appearance of caring for the sheep, but he would flee if there was any danger. The Good Shepherd is altogether different. He knows His sheep, and He calls them by name. His sheep hear His voice and respond to His call. The Good Shepherd lays down His life for His sheep. He selflessly loves and cares for His own. This passage has much to teach us about the nature of Christ's sacrifice. He did not lose His life; He gave it for His own. He humbly and sacrificially gave His very life so that He might save His people.

The passage also speaks of other sheep who are not of this fold. Here, Jesus is speaking of those outside the nation of Israel. God's plan has always been to call His own from every tribe and nation of the earth. Jesus speaks here of the Gentiles and proclaims that salvation will go out to His sheep from every nation. This was beautifully pictured in Ezekiel 34:11-16. God seeks out His sheep from every nation. He runs after them when they are lost and helpless. He leaves the 99 to go after the one that is lost. He pursues His own wherever they are, and He brings them to Himself. Jesus runs after the broken, the lonely, and the sinner, and He brings them home to Himself. Revelation 7:9-10 provides a picture of this truth as we see the redeemed of all ages and nations worshiping their Savior forever.

As Jesus finished speaking, many believed, but many were simply confused by His words. What kind of man was this? How could He speak with such authority and power? Was Jesus who He said He was?

These words overflow with hope for our hearts today. Jesus is still the Good Shepherd. He still tenderly guides us and provides our needs. The promise of His presence still rests with us today. And abundant life is found in Him alone. It is Jesus who has laid down His life for His own, and now we rest in the life that He has provided. Our Good Shepherd will never leave us alone. He will walk with us, strengthen us, and guide us until the day He brings us home.

DAY 2 QUESTIONS

1. PSALM 23 IS ONE OF THE MOST FAMOUS PASSAGES THAT POINTS TO GOD AS SHEPHERD. LOOK AT TODAY'S PASSAGE AS WELL AS PSALM 23 AND RECORD WHAT YOU LEARN ABOUT THE GOOD SHEPHERD.

JOHN 10:7-21	PSALM 23

2. WHAT DO YOU THINK IT MEANS TO HAVE ABUNDANT LIFE?

3. HOW DOES THIS PASSAGE ENCOURAGE YOU TO LOOK TO JESUS AND TRUST HIS GUIDANCE?

WEEK 6 DAY 3

> WE WILL BE PRESERVED BECAUSE HE IS THE ONE WHO PRESERVES US. HIS GRIP IS STRONG, AND HE WILL NOT LET GO.

HE WILL NEVER LET GO

READ: JOHN 10:22-42

As Jesus's ministry continued, it seemed that the opposition continued to grow stronger and stronger. Today's passage opens not at the Feast of Booths or Feast of Tabernacles, but several weeks later at the Feast of Dedication. This feast was not one of the prescribed feasts in the Old Testament law but instead had come about during the time between the Old and New Testaments in what we would call the intertestamental period. This feast was in commemoration of the revolt against Antiochus Epiphanes led by Judas Maccabaeus. This feast is what we would commonly refer to as Hanukkah. John sets the scene by telling us that it was winter, but his description is telling of more than just the cold temperatures. It also shows us the state of the cold hearts of those who refused to believe.

The Jews gathered around Jesus, and from their words it seemed like they wanted to know who Jesus was and believe in Him. But Jesus had told them and shown them that He was the Messiah, and they had refused to acknowledge this truth. They claimed to want to believe, but truly they had come to condemn Him.

The people of God are called by God and kept by God.

Jesus explained that His works revealed who He was and then returned to His illustration of the sheep and a shepherd. The sheep hear and know the voice of their Good Shepherd. They are given eternal life, and they are forever secure. The words of Jesus here speak of the eternal security of all believers. The people of God are called by God and kept by God. Jesus declared for them the hope of the gospel and the matchless gift of God's grace, but they refused to hear.

When Jesus claimed oneness with the Father, the Jews picked up their stones to stone Him, but His time had not yet come. There was still work to be done, and God's plan would not be thwarted. Jesus pointed them to the miraculous works that He had done, but they would not hear it. Just here in the book of John we have seen Jesus turn water to wine, cleanse the temple, heal the sick and the blind, feed thousands, walk on water, and proclaim the hope of the Messiah. But the people would not listen. Jesus tried to show them that His works and His word declared who He was, but they refused to hear. Their eyes were blinded, and their ears were shut to the Messiah before their own eyes. They wanted to ignore His works, and they were angered by His words. They dug in their heels and refused to believe. They were proving His point; they were not of His flock.

They wanted to arrest Him, but He escaped. It was not yet His hour. The text tells us that He went across the Jordan. While in Jerusalem, the people had sought to stone and arrest Him, but here was totally different. Here, many believed in His name. They saw what He had done, they heard His word, and they believed. Jesus had pursued His sheep, and they had heard His voice. The presence of Jesus demanded a response. Hear and remain in unbelief, or hear and believe. But the promise was sure — all who had been given to Him by the Father would believe.

To the people of God, these words should bring us peace and rest in the Lord. These verses are a reminder of the gospel of grace to those who have been saved by grace. God will not fail His children. As the people of God, we have been called by God, and we can rest in knowing that we will be kept by God. We will be preserved because He is the One who preserves us. His grip is strong, and He will not let go. Nothing in this world is secure, and everything in this world can be lost. But Jesus shifts our gaze from the things we can lose to the things that can never be lost. We may lose position and wealth. We may lose relationships and even family. We may lose everything in this world, but we will never lose Jesus, because He will never lose us.

DAY 3 QUESTIONS

1. WHAT DO YOU THINK JESUS SAID IN THIS PASSAGE THAT MOST ANGERED THOSE WHO REFUSED TO BELIEVE?

2. WHAT DOES THIS PASSAGE TEACH US ABOUT THE GOSPEL?

3. READ ROMANS 8:31-39. HOW DOES GOD'S STEADFAST GRIP ON YOU ENCOURAGE YOU TO PRESS FORWARD? IS THERE A SPECIFIC AREA OF YOUR LIFE WHERE YOU NEEDED THIS REMINDER?

WEEK 6 DAY 4

"

HOPE IS FOUND IN WHO HE IS.

THE RESURRECTION AND THE LIFE

READ: JOHN 11:1-27

CROSS REFERENCE:

1 Peter 5:7

Chapter 11 opens with the news that one of Jesus's dearest friends is ill. Jesus was not nearby when he became ill, but his sisters Mary and Martha sent word to Jesus for help. They appeal to Jesus for help based on Jesus's love. They did not ask Him to help because of their great love for Him, but because of His great love for others. This family had been disciples and dear friends of Jesus in His ministry. They had seen His miracles. They knew that He could heal the sick, and they knew that He loved them. Surely, He would heal such a close friend.

Jesus's response was that this illness would not lead to death but that God and the Son of God would be glorified through it. The words of this passage are perplexing from a limited, human perspective. Jesus loved them, yet He stayed where He was for two more days. Most people are not particularly fond of waiting, especially in difficult circumstances. When Mary and Martha asked for Jesus's help, they expected Him to answer their request immediately, but instead they waited. When Jesus said that Lazarus was sleeping, the disciples did not even understand what He meant until Jesus plainly told them that Lazarus had died.

"I am the resurrection and the life."

When Jesus finally arrived, Lazarus had already been dead for four days. He had been placed in the tomb. The mourners had come. It seemed all hope was lost. Martha was the first to run out to meet Him with the words, "Lord, if you had been here, my brother would not have died." She believed in Jesus with every fiber of her being. She had seen what He could do. She had heard Him teach. She knew that if He had come, He could have healed her brother. Her heart was full of questions, but it was also full of faith. Jesus told her that her brother would rise again, and it was revealed that she was resting in that. She knew that someday, on the last day, her brother would rise again. But the promise of the future still left her with questions in the present.

Jesus responded with powerful words in the fifth "I Am" statement when He declared, "I am the resurrection and the life." The promise of comfort and hope for the weeping and the mourning were not found in anything other than who Jesus is. Resurrection and life are not something that Jesus simply does or simply gives; this is who Jesus is. We do not wait until after death to experience eternal life; we have a taste of it right now because it is who He is, and He is with us. Hope is found in who He is. Her response was belief. She still did not understand, but she believed Him.

Sometimes delays are part of the plan. Sometimes God calls His people to wait. Sometimes it seems like prayer requests have gone unanswered. Yet, we can rest in this same truth that He is good and gracious and that He will do what is best. Delays cannot dissolve His plan. Delays are part of His plan. They are not delays to Him.

Lord, if you _____. How often have we felt this phrase in our hearts? Perhaps we do not even say it out loud, but the ache of our hearts affirms it. We know God is all-powerful. We know He could take away our heartache. And sometimes we wonder why He does not. But Scripture gives us space to lament. It gives us space to ask questions and take our burdens to the Lord. In 1 Peter 5:7, we are commanded to bring our anxieties to the Lord and cast them on Him. The Psalms overflow with raw emotion and questions to the Lord. He is not offended by our questions. He desires us to come. And yet, we can also rest in the concrete truth that He is the answer to our questions. The answer to our troubles is not for our problems to go away. The answer is found in who He is. He is the God who restores. He is the God who brings beauty from ashes. Comfort for our hearts is found in who He is.

He is the resurrection and the life. He is the giver and sustainer of life. He is life itself, and there is no life apart from Him. Death and sorrow abound in a broken world, but Jesus is with us. The resurrection and the life dwells within every redeemed child of God. We have hope because we have Jesus. Our lives are in His hands, and there is no safer place for them to be. Sorrow and suffering leave us confused and questioning, but His call to us is to come and find rest in Him.

DAY 4 QUESTIONS

1. HAS THERE EVER BEEN A SITUATION IN YOUR LIFE WHEN YOU HAVE QUESTIONED WHY GOD DID NOT INTERVENE? HOW DOES THIS PASSAGE ENCOURAGE YOU?

2. WHY SHOULD IT ENCOURAGE US THAT JESUS IS THE RESURRECTION AND THE LIFE?

3. WHAT DOES IT MEAN TO FIND LIFE AND REST IN JESUS?

WEEK 6 DAY 5

"

FOR GENERATIONS, DEATH HAD ALWAYS BEEN VICTORIOUS. BUT JESUS HAD COME TO DESTROY THE POWER OF DEATH.

JESUS WEPT

READ: JOHN 11:28-44

CROSS REFERENCE:

Romans 12:15

Ephesians 2:4-10

Just a moment after Jesus uttered the fifth "I Am" statement to Martha, she went and called her sister Mary. Mary did not delay. As soon as she knew Jesus was there and was asking for her, she immediately got up and went to meet Him. When she came to Him, she fell at His feet. It is interesting to note that every time Mary is found in Scripture, we see her at the feet of Jesus. It may seem to us to be a contradiction that she is at the feet of Jesus and is pouring out her heart and questions to Him. Her words echo the words of her sister, "Lord, if you had only been here." Her mind and heart must have been reeling as she looked in the eyes of Jesus. She knew that He loved them. She knew that He was the Lord. She knew that He could have done something. She knew He could have healed her brother and removed her pain.

The crowds around did not help. While some saw Jesus's deep love for His friends and disciples, others scoffed during this family's time of grief. Their mocking voices declared that if Jesus was who He said He was, surely He could have kept the man from dying. If He could heal the blind, why did not He heal His own friend? Their skeptical and cynical hearts spoke words of pain into a tender moment. Their sharp remarks likely wounded the grieving sisters.

The Son of God, the Sovereign King, the Savior of the world wept.

The text tells us that Jesus was deeply moved with compassion. His heart was breaking over their sorrow. His holy wrath was kindled by the insensitive crowd. He asked to see where Lazarus had been placed. Verse 35 is the shortest verse in the English Bible, and yet within these two words is truth that could fill volumes of writing. Jesus wept. The Son of God, the Sovereign King, the Savior of the world wept. We see here a picture in just a few words of the mystery of the incarnation. Jesus is fully

God and fully man. He was not immune to the dust of the winding roads of Bethany that collected in His sandals. He was not exempt from the pains of hunger or the ache of exhaustion. And this Jesus was not far off from the anguish of grief.

He knew the end of the story. He knew that Lazarus would not be dead for long. Yet He wept. He wept because this is life in a fallen world. Death seems to have the final victory. This is the way that it had been since Adam and Eve were sent out of the garden. For generations, death had always been victorious. But Jesus had come to destroy the power of death. The defeat of death would not take place until a few chapters later outside the city of Jerusalem, but Jesus's friends would see a glimpse of it this day. He wept because His friends did not know the end of the story. They looked ahead to no end of the grief that they were facing. With a glimmer of faith, they awaited a final resurrection, but right now, hope seemed lost. Their hearts were overwhelmed with sorrow and grief, and Jesus entered in. He did not insulate Himself from their sorrow. He did not scoff at their suffering. He drew near to them. He saw them. He loved them.

Moved by compassion, He went to the tomb and made an unthinkable request. He commanded that the stone be rolled away. Martha was likely horrified as she reminded Jesus of how long Lazarus had been in the tomb. After four days, the odor would have been unbearable. But Jesus reminded her of His words, and despite the taboo nature of the request, the stone was rolled away. Jesus prayed for all to hear and then lifted His voice and called Lazarus out of the grave. As Lazarus walked out of the cold tomb, the glory of God was on display. This Jesus was a man who wept with compassion for His friends, but He was so much more. Death bowed at the sound of His voice. For generations, death had seemed to have the final say, but Jesus declared that death would be forever defeated. The cross would have the final say.

This passage teaches us about who Jesus is and what He came to do. It gives us space to ask our own questions and cry out to a God who is deeply moved by our own sorrows and suffering. Though He knows the end of the story, He weeps for our pain and intercedes to the Father for us. He is our greatest example of one who weeps with those who weep (Romans 12:15). As we walk through our lives we can rest in the knowledge that no matter what we are facing, Jesus is the answer. Hope is found only in Him.

We may be asking the same questions as we reflect on things in our lives. Why does God allow it? Why does not He step in? Is there a limit to Jesus's power? Is my situation out of His control? Perhaps we would not even say the words out loud. Perhaps the words written in our prayer journals have been adjusted to sound more acceptable. Yet through it all we can rest in the sovereign hand of a loving Savior who is moved with compassion in our need. He knows the end of our story. He knows that there will be a day when death and sin will be forever defeated. But He also knows the pain that overwhelms our hearts right now. He is moved with compassion. He is motivated by love. He sees us. He comes to us. He is working for us, even when we cannot see the ways that He is working. He is working, when all we see is waiting. When all we see is struggle, He is steadfast and sure. And as His word called Lazarus from death to life, He has called His own out of the grave of their sin (Ephesians 2:4-10). He calls us to come and believe, come and drink the waters of life, and come and rest in His love.

DAY 5 QUESTIONS

1   WHAT DO WE LEARN ABOUT JESUS IN THIS PASSAGE?

2   WHY DO YOU THINK WE ARE SOMETIMES AFRAID TO ASK GOD THE QUESTIONS THAT ARE ON OUR HEARTS? TAKE YOUR STRUGGLES, FEARS, AND QUESTIONS TO THE LORD.

3   WHAT DOES THIS PASSAGE ALONG WITH ROMANS 12:15 TEACH US ABOUT HOW WE SHOULD RESPOND TO OTHERS WHEN THEY ARE HURTING?

WEEK 6
SCRIPTURE MEMORY

JOHN 1:10-11

He was in the world, and the world was created through him, and yet the world did not recognize him. He came to his own, and his own people did not receive him.

WEEK SIX
REFLECTION

REVIEW
John 10:1 – 11:44

PARAPHRASE THE PASSAGE FROM THIS WEEK.

WHAT DID YOU OBSERVE FROM THIS WEEK'S TEXT ABOUT GOD AND HIS CHARACTER?

WHAT DOES THIS WEEK'S PASSAGE REVEAL ABOUT THE CONDITION OF MANKIND AND YOURSELF?

HOW DOES THIS PASSAGE POINT TO THE GOSPEL?

HOW SHOULD YOU RESPOND TO THIS PASSAGE? WHAT SPECIFIC ACTION STEPS CAN YOU TAKE THIS WEEK TO APPLY THIS PASSAGE?

WRITE A PRAYER OF RESPONSE TO YOUR STUDY OF GOD'S WORD.

Adore God for who He is, confess sins that He revealed in your own life, ask Him to empower you to walk in obedience, and pray for anyone who comes to mind as you study.

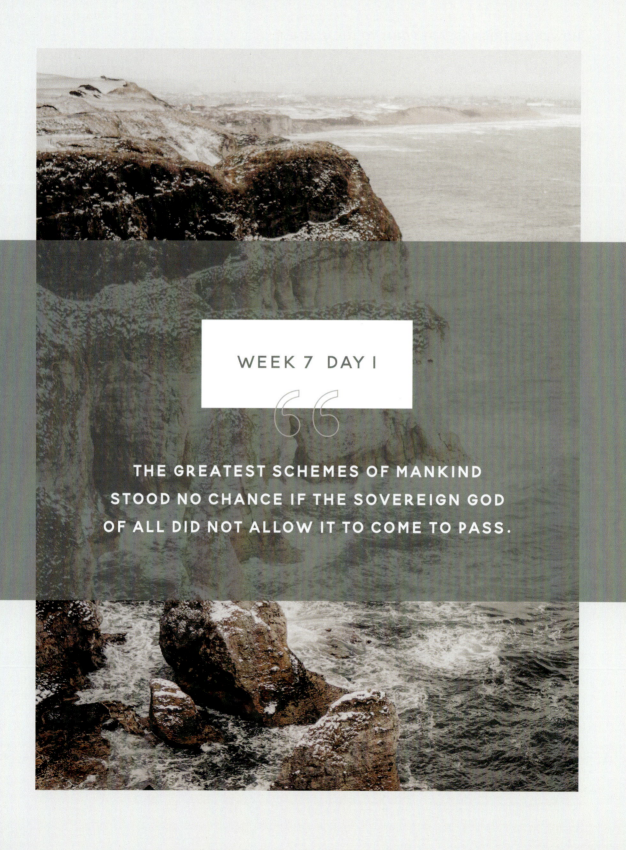

WEEK 7 DAY 1

"

THE GREATEST SCHEMES OF MANKIND STOOD NO CHANCE IF THE SOVEREIGN GOD OF ALL DID NOT ALLOW IT TO COME TO PASS.

TO GATHER THE CHILDREN OF GOD

READ: JOHN 11:45-57

CROSS REFERENCE:

Acts 2:23

Proverbs 19:21

Many watched on as Jesus raised a man from death to life. A man who had once been dead was now alive, and again it prompted an evaluation of who Jesus is. Today's text opens with the news that many who had seen what Jesus did had believed. Jesus had declared Himself to be the resurrection and the life, and they saw the proof of this truth before their eyes. Many believed that He could raise them too. Those dead in their sins found life in Jesus.

While many believed, there were others who were hardened in their sin. They came to the Pharisees to tell what Jesus had done. The council referred to here is the Sanhedrin, Israel's highest judiciary. The accusations about Jesus are perplexing. No one denied the miracles Jesus had done or even that He had raised Lazarus from the dead. Their accusation was that people would believe in Him, and they did not want this to happen. The last thing that they wanted was a man named Jesus to threaten their political power and authority over the people.

Those dead in their sins found life in Jesus.

Caiaphas was the high priest that year, and he stepped forward with his own contribution to the discussion. The words he spoke were far more prophetic than he could have even realized. He looked at the situation and said that it would be better for Jesus to die than for the whole nation to be destroyed. His solution was to stop the threat, and he saw Jesus as the threat. And yet, a closer look at the words he spoke reveal a glimpse into the sovereign plan of God. Jesus would die. He would die in the place of sinners who despised and rejected Him. He would die to redeem His own. Caiaphas's words give us a stunning picture of one of Christianity's most foundational doctrines—substitutionary atonement. These words spoken at the time of Passover presented Jesus as the Passover Lamb. He would die in the place of those He came to redeem. His blood would be shed, not just for those who would believe from the nation of Israel but also for all the children of God around the world—and even for those in the distant future who would believe on His name.

The temptation may be to look at this passage and rest the sacrifice of Jesus on the shoulders of Caiaphas. Caiaphas is completely responsible for his actions, but God was not taken off guard by Caiaphas's devious and horrific plan. God did not scramble to keep up with the errant will of sinful humanity. Before time began, Calvary had been the plan. Over and over in the book of John, we have seen mention of Jesus's hour. Try as they might to kill Him or run Him out of town, the attempts of the religious leaders to stifle the ministry of Christ would not be effective until God allowed it to be. The greatest schemes of mankind stood no chance if the sovereign God of all did not allow it to come to pass. Acts 2:23 reminds us that Jesus was delivered up to be killed according to the definite plan and the sovereign foreknowledge of God. He was delivered into the hands of evil men but only because God allowed it.

In love, the Father offered His Son as a sacrifice for everyone Jesus came to redeem. This sacrifice was willing and intentional. In love the Father initiated a plan of salvation, in love the Son graciously secured that salvation, and in love the Spirit applies it to the hearts of all who believe. God's plan would not be thwarted, and His promises would stand. Jesus had come to rescue and redeem, and indeed He would.

The people of God can find comfort in knowing that Jesus came to save His own. The people of God can rest in the knowledge that God's plan cannot be thwarted. We can rest in the knowledge that the same sovereign God who would not allow a hand to be placed on Jesus before the appointed time, will not allow anything to happen to us that is outside the scope of His divine plan. Child of God, you are in Christ. There is no more secure place to be than in Christ, and there is nothing that you can do to fall out of His grip of grace. Many are the plans of the wicked, but God's plan will come to pass (Proverbs 19:21). Every child of God can rest his or her heart on that steadfast truth.

DAY 7 QUESTIONS

1   READ ACTS 2:23. WHAT DO THIS VERSE AND TODAY'S PASSAGE TEACH YOU ABOUT GOD'S PLAN?

2   READ PROVERBS 19:21 AND THINK ABOUT TODAY'S PASSAGE AND YOUR OWN LIFE. HOW DO YOU FIND COMFORT IN THIS VERSE?

3   WHAT DO YOU NEED TO TRUST THE LORD FOR TODAY? HOW CAN YOU REST IN HIS PLAN, EVEN WHEN IT DOES NOT MAKE SENSE?

WEEK 7 DAY 2

"

AS THE PEOPLE OF GOD, WE SHOULD
POUR OUT OUR LIVES, OUR RESOURCES,
AND EVERY SINGLE PART OF OURSELVES
IN SERVICE TO JESUS.

EXTRAVAGANT DEVOTION

READ: JOHN 12:1-11

As we move into chapter 12, we also move into Jesus's final week. John spends nearly half of this Gospel on this final passion week. While all of the Gospels pay specific attention to the events of this final week, John's approach is slightly different than the other Gospel writers. While the other Gospels focus on the public ministry of Jesus during this time, John focuses on His personal interactions. We see that clearly displayed here as we see Jesus return to Bethany just a few days before Passover began. He came back for dinner with His dear friends Lazarus, Mary, and Martha.

While the Jews were plotting to arrest Jesus, Jesus had returned to rejoice with His friend. It would not be long, as we see at the end of the passage, until the Jews would be plotting to kill Lazarus as well. They could not have such a visible demonstration of the power of Jesus walking, breathing, and living among the people. Martha was busy serving the meal, and Jesus and Lazarus were reclined at the table that was low to the ground. Mary took a pound of expensive ointment perfume to anoint Jesus. The value of this fragrant offering was a year's wages for the common worker. Her gift was extravagant and generous. Her offering was humble and devoted. Culturally, it was taboo for her to let down her hair. Woman were required to keep their hair up in all social settings. It would only be in extremely intimate settings that a

> Her gift was extravagant and generous.
> Her offering was humble and devoted.

woman would be permitted to take down her hair. A married woman could be divorced and a single woman could be stoned for such a scandalous act. Yet Mary, like Jesus often did, defied the social norms. This is seen in her humility as well. Even servants were often exempt from washing the dirty feet of their masters. It was seen as the lowest duty one could have. But willingly, Mary lowered herself. She did not just wash His feet, but she washed them with her hair.

Mary is seen several times throughout the Gospels, and every time, she is seen at the feet of Jesus. Her love, gratitude, and worship for Him compelled her to display her extravagant devotion. The text says that she was anointing Him for burial. It seems that Mary, and perhaps Mary alone, was aware of what was ahead. Jesus would die for the sins of His people and would conquer death once and for all.

Immediately, there was pushback. Here in John, we see it from Judas, but other accounts imply that other disciples may have had similar concerns. This gift was certainly extravagant. She had poured out an expensive treasure. Could this not have been sold and the money given to the poor? While several of the disciples may have questioned her actions or motivations, John tells us the reason for Judas's questions. He was a thief, and he desired this money to line his own pockets.

Jesus immediately rebukes the dissenters, affirming what Mary had done. In no way was Jesus neglecting to give to the poor. In fact, Jesus's ministry had focused greatly on the poor and rebuking the religious leaders for their mistreatment of the vulnerable and oppressed. Jesus was telling them that He would not always be there. Something was coming, and He would be leaving. Mary's sacrifice of extravagant love was good and honorable.

Mary's attitude and actions should be an example to us. We serve the same Jesus for whom she poured out her greatest treasure, and it is instructive to us to see the actions Christ honored. As the people of God, we should pour out our lives, our resources, and every single part of ourselves in service to Jesus. We should humble ourselves before Him as He has humbled Himself to redeem us. We should expect that there will be times when our actions and motives will be questioned, even by other believers, and we should seek the glory of Christ above all else. We live to serve Jesus alone, and every part of our lives should be in worship to His name.

DAY 2 QUESTIONS

1. WHAT DOES THIS PASSAGE TEACH YOU ABOUT HOW YOU SHOULD RESPOND TO JESUS?

2. READ ROMANS 12:1. WHAT DOES IT MEAN FOR OUR LIVES TO BE LIVING SACRIFICES?

3. JESUS IS WORTHY OF EVERYTHING THAT WE HAVE. HOW CAN YOU PRACTICALLY APPLY THIS PASSAGE THIS WEEK?

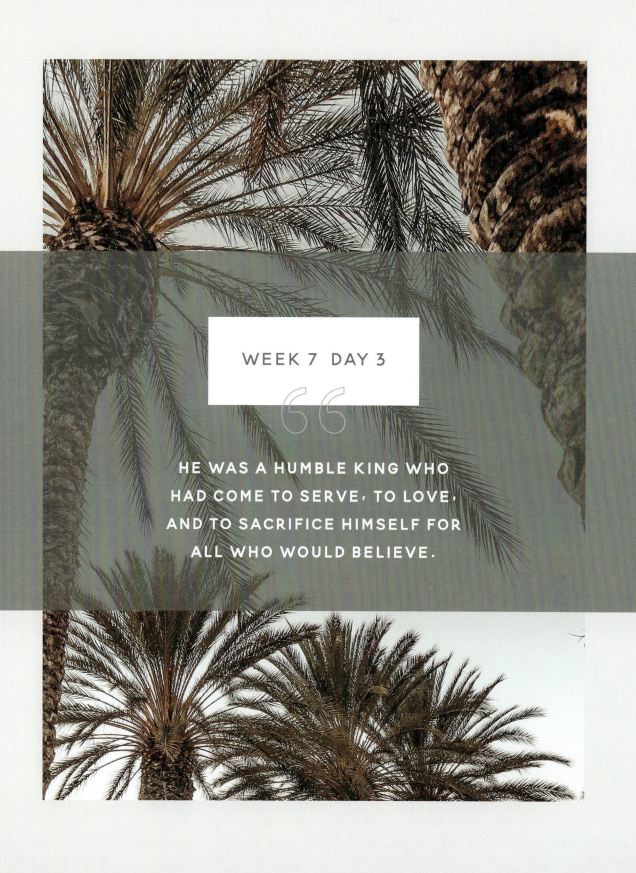

WEEK 7 DAY 3

"

HE WAS A HUMBLE KING WHO
HAD COME TO SERVE, TO LOVE,
AND TO SACRIFICE HIMSELF FOR
ALL WHO WOULD BELIEVE.

HOSANNA

READ: JOHN 12:12-26

CROSS REFERENCE:

Psalm 118:25-26
Zechariah 9:9-10

The triumphal entry of Jesus is one of the most beloved passages of Scripture. It is one of just a few accounts from Jesus's life and ministry that is recorded in all four Gospels. It is celebrated each year around the world as believers celebrate the Sunday before Easter on what is commonly referred to as Palm Sunday. The city of Jerusalem was bustling with throngs of people coming into the city for the Passover. Jesus and the disciples were among the crowds coming for the Passover feast. Word had spread quickly about Jesus, and all eyes were on Him. The news of the resurrection of Lazarus was on everyone's lips, and the questions of Jesus's identity peppered countless conversations. When they heard Jesus was coming into the city, they sprang to action and came to meet Him.

Whether due to the events in Bethany when Lazarus was raised from the dead or due to some nationalistic zeal, the people had recognized Jesus as the Messiah. But sadly, their understanding of who the Messiah would be was confused and mistaken. They were looking for a conquering king and a great political ruler.

Hosanna meant save us, and that is exactly what He had come to do.

They longed for one who would crush the power of Rome and restore Israel to her glory days. They sang the words of Psalm 118:25-26 as they shouted Hosanna. They lifted their palm branches which were symbols of nationalism, revolution, worship, and victory. As their voices lifted with the cry of Hosanna, they did not fully understand the words that came from their lips. Hosanna meant "save us," and that is exactly what He had come to do. They were looking for a political savior, but He had come to rescue their hearts. Their enemy was much stronger than the powers of Rome; it was the curse of sin and death. And Jesus was the only One who could rescue them from their greatest enemy.

But Jesus stopped before coming to the procession and found a young donkey. He was fulfilling the prophecy of Zechariah 9:9, and He was proclaiming that He was a different kind of king. He was not a tyrannical military leader who rode up on a stallion or warhorse. He was a humble king who had come to serve, to love, and to sacrifice Himself for all who would believe. He was the King of Israel, but He was also the King of all the world and the King of peace just as Zechariah 9:9-10 had declared generations before. He was the King. He was the King above all other kings.

The Pharisees scoffed among themselves saying that the whole world was seeking to follow after Him. While their statements were an over-exaggeration, it was true that Jesus had come to rescue more than just the people of national Israel. In the very next verses, we see some coming to worship who were Greeks and had been converted to Judaism. They came to Philip and said that they wanted to see Jesus. Surely, they had heard of this man unlike any other man, and now they desired to meet Him for themselves.

Over and over throughout the book of John, Jesus has declared that His hour had not yet come. But now, something is different. Jesus declared the hour had come. It was time for Him to be glorified. And this glorification would take place in the most unexpected way. It would not be in a palace, as a military leader, or on a throne of gold. His throne would be the cross.

This is what all of history had been building toward. Jesus had come to die. He had come to go to the cross, and the bloody cross would not be defeat but victory.

The call of Jesus to those listening that day, and to every believer, is this—follow me. The call is not one of success and achievement but one of humility and sacrifice. This is a call to die. As Christ has died for us, so we too are to die to the world and our own plans and dreams. But the call to follow Him is accompanied by a promise. He will be with all those who follow Him. He will not leave them alone. In laying down our lives for Christ, we gain Christ, and there is no greater treasure that we could ask for. He is the reward. He is the reason we live.

Hosanna is who He is. He is the One who has come to rescue and redeem. He lived the life we could not live, and He died the death that we deserve. He came to go to the cross. He is our King. May the plea of our hearts be a desire to see Jesus. May every moment of our lives be a demonstration of what it means to follow Him. And through it all, may we carry with us the promise of His presence, which is the greatest gift of all.

DAY 3 QUESTIONS

1. HOW WAS JESUS MISUNDERSTOOD IN THIS PASSAGE? HOW IS HE MISUNDERSTOOD TODAY?

2. WHAT DOES IT MEAN TO FOLLOW JESUS?

3. IN WHAT WAY DO YOU NEED TO FOLLOW JESUS TODAY?

WEEK 7 DAY 4

> "
>
> JESUS KNEW THIS WAS THE REASON THAT HE HAD COME. JESUS CAME TO DIE. HE CAME TO BRING GLORY TO THE FATHER.

FOR THE GLORY OF THE FATHER

READ: JOHN 12:27-50

CROSS REFERENCE:

John 3:14-15

The close of chapter 12 also closes this entire section of the book of John that is often referred to as The Book of Signs. The rest of the book will be a detailed unfolding of the Passion Week. But John does not conclude this section without first giving readers a glimpse once again into the heart of Jesus and the reason He came.

The book of John does not record the agony of Jesus in the garden of Gethsemane, but many of the same emotions that are expressed in that scene are demonstrated for us right here in this passage. Jesus was troubled. He knew what was coming. The cross was the cruelest death that could be imagined, and He knew that it would soon be the cup that He would drink. We see a beautiful picture here of the humanity of Christ and His anguish over the bitter cup that He must drink. What lay ahead would be brutal and painful, and yet Jesus knew this was the reason that He had come. Jesus came to die. He came to bring glory to the Father. The Father's reassuring voice thundered from heaven. The Father's name would be glorified in the Son's obedience, and the children of God would be brought near through sacrifice.

Jesus is the way to God. And the Word of God is the way to Jesus.

The Son of Man would be lifted up just as Jesus had told Nicodemus in John 3:14-15. And by being lifted up, the children of God from every tribe, tongue, and nation would be drawn to God. This passage does not teach that all people will accept Christ, but that the message of salvation would go out to all kinds of people. The Messiah had not come for the Jews alone. He had come for Samaritan women sitting at wells. He had come for Greeks who wanted to know Him. The people of God were not only from Israel but from every place on earth. Jesus is the way to God. And the Word of God is the way to Jesus. This gospel message would be proclaimed to all the world, and the chosen of God would find hope in the words of the gospel.

Jesus had demonstrated in every possible way that He was the Messiah and the Savior of the world. He had worked miracles, fulfilled promises, and transformed the lives of those who believed. And many did believe as John has chronicled. But still there were those who refused to see who Jesus was. For them, unbelief was not just the state of their minds but also the state of their hearts. They refused to see what was in front of them. Their pride and self-sufficiency would not allow them to see the One who had come to rescue and redeem. Yet John reminds us that this was not a surprise to God. In fact, their unbelief was prophesied by Isaiah generations before. They were so blinded in their sin that they could not believe. Faith is never something that we muster up in our own strength. Faith is a gift from the Lord. And without Him opening the eyes of the blind, none would ever believe. Verse 43 tells us that they loved the glory that comes from man more than the glory that comes from God. This sobering observation is a commentary on the human condition. But this is why Jesus came—to show a better way. He came to show that life begins when we lay down our lives and follow Him.

Jesus cried out with the call to believe. He called for sinners, poor and needy, to come to Him. Yet, many could not recognize that this was their condition. Jesus came to call His own from darkness to light. He did not come to judge but to restore. He came with the authority of the Father and the love demonstrated by sacrifice. Jesus came to save.

Jesus came to save, and He came to make us like Him. Today's passage is instructional for us as we grow in godliness. Jesus was not exempt from anguish, and neither are we. We will face the troubles of life in a fallen world. But like Him, we can learn where to go when things burden our hearts. Jesus went to the Father in prayer, and because of what Jesus has done, we have the privilege to do the same. We can go to the Lord with every burden that is on our hearts and know that He will hear His own. We also learn from Jesus the purpose of our lives. The glory of God was why Jesus came, and it is why we are here as well. Every moment of our lives can be lived for His glory. Even our pain and suffering can be redeemed by our God. We must heed the warning of Christ not to live as those who persisted in unbelief and craved the approval of man rather than the glory of God. The purpose of our lives is His glory. May we keep this central in every hour of every day. Jesus came as the Light of the world, and now our heart's desire must be to point people to the light.

DAY 4 QUESTIONS

1   WHAT DOES THIS PASSAGE TEACH YOU ABOUT WHO JESUS IS?

2   WHAT DOES THIS PASSAGE TEACH YOU ABOUT HOW YOU CAN BE MORE LIKE JESUS?

3   HOW CAN YOU PRACTICALLY LIVE EVERY PART OF YOUR LIFE FOR THE GLORY OF GOD?

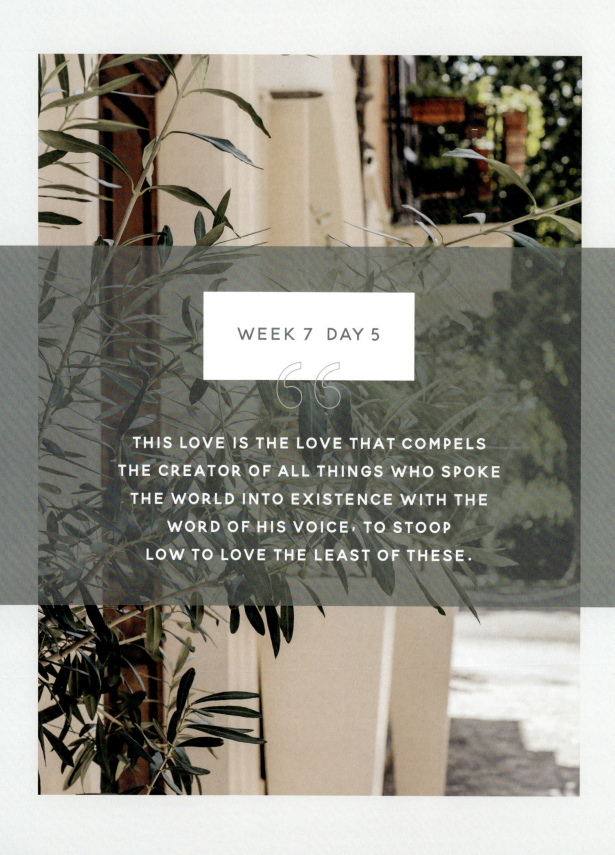

WEEK 7 DAY 5

"

THIS LOVE IS THE LOVE THAT COMPELS THE CREATOR OF ALL THINGS WHO SPOKE THE WORLD INTO EXISTENCE WITH THE WORD OF HIS VOICE, TO STOOP LOW TO LOVE THE LEAST OF THESE.

LOVED TO THE END

READ: JOHN 13:1-20

CROSS REFERENCE:

Philippians 2

The second half of the book of John begins by reminding us what is about to happen. The hour has come. The time of Jesus's crucifixion is drawing near. Yet these words are accompanied with a powerful declaration of the love of Jesus for His own. Throughout the book of John, there has been a great emphasis on Jesus's love for the world, but the second half of this Gospel will share intimate details about His love for His own. These final chapters give us immense insight into the relationship between the disciples and Jesus and ultimately between any child of God and their Savior.

The actions and motivations of Jesus are rooted in love. He loves His people. Verse 1 tells us that He loved them to the end. This can reference both the length of His love in that He loved them until He took His final breath on the cross, and also to the depth of His love, He loved them with everything He is. This is supernatural love. It is selfless and sacrificial. This love is the love that compels the Creator of all things who spoke the world into existence with the word of His voice, to stoop low to love the least

> The actions and motivations of Jesus are rooted in love.

of these. It is the love that compels the Lord of all to humble Himself to the place of a servant (Philippians 2). And perhaps nowhere other than the cross itself is Jesus's humility seen more than in these verses.

It is here that we see Jesus humble Himself to the most menial task. We are not given a ton of description of the scene. The disciples were gathering for the Passover feast, the meal that would become known as the Last Supper. In the culture, there was traditionally a servant who would wash the feet of those attending the event. This dirty and humiliating task was reserved for the lowest in the social order. Even Jewish slaves were exempt from this disgusting duty. It was reserved for Gentile slaves. But there was no servant to be found. Perhaps the disciples were frustrated by the oversight at such an important gathering. Perhaps they tried to stay out of the way, fearing that they may be summoned to complete the necessary but humiliating task. And then it happened. Jesus got up from the table and took off His outer garments. He tied a towel around Himself and knelt down and began washing the feet of His disciples. They must have been so shocked that no one said a word—just watching Him in stunned silence with no sound but the water that poured into the basin.

Then He came to Peter. Peter had never been one to stay silent. And it seems Peter could not get over how inappropriate he found this to be. So, he objected, but Jesus stopped him. Peter did not understand what was happening, but Jesus told him that without being washed, he would have no share with Jesus. Peter begged for Jesus to wash not just his feet but every part of him. However, Jesus clearly pointed out that not everyone in that room was clean. There was one who would very shortly be the one to betray Jesus.

What Jesus was doing was so much more than washing the dirty feet of His disciples. He was providing a picture for them to see. It was not about foot washing but about the sacrifice that had the power to make people clean. Without being cleansed by Jesus, no one would have a share with Him. This cleansing was pointing to a far greater cleansing that was about to take place. Jesus's death on the cross would be fueled by love, humility, sacrifice, and take place in the sovereign timing of the Father.

Throughout the Gospel of John is the call of Jesus to follow him. This passage is no different. It is a call for the children of God to follow in the way that Jesus walked. It is a call to come to Him for cleansing and then serve one another. It is a call to humility and radical service, not as a way to earn the love of God but as a response to the love that was demonstrated to us on the cross of Christ. We are people of pride and selfishness. We push against any service that we think is below us. But Jesus teaches us that service is holy and sacred. Serving others is a way of demonstrating the love of the Father to our brothers and sisters in the faith and to the world around us. Jesus served in ways that seemed insignificant and mundane, and He teaches us that everything we do is an act of worship to the One who has served us. The way of Jesus is backwards to this world. His kingdom is an upside-down kingdom. In His kingdom, humility, and service are rewarded because they are marks of hearts transformed by the gospel of grace.

DAY 5 QUESTIONS

1. WHAT DOES THIS PASSAGE TEACH US ABOUT HOW JESUS RELATES TO HIS DISCIPLES?

2. HOW DOES THIS PASSAGE HELP US TO UNDERSTAND HOW WE SHOULD VIEW HUMILITY AND SERVICE IN OUR OWN LIVES?

3. JESUS OFTEN USES THE PHRASE, "FOLLOW ME." WHAT DOES IT MEAN TO FOLLOW HIM, AND HOW CAN YOU GROW PERSONALLY IN FOLLOWING JESUS?

WEEK 7
SCRIPTURE MEMORY

JOHN 1:12-13

But to all who did receive him, he gave them the right to be children of God, to those who believe in his name, who were born, not of natural descent, or of the will of the flesh, or of the will of man, but of God.

WEEK SEVEN REFLECTION

REVIEW
John 11:45 – 13:20

PARAPHRASE THE PASSAGE FROM THIS WEEK.

WHAT DID YOU OBSERVE FROM THIS WEEK'S TEXT ABOUT GOD AND HIS CHARACTER?

WHAT DOES THIS WEEK'S PASSAGE REVEAL ABOUT THE CONDITION OF MANKIND AND YOURSELF?

HOW DOES THIS PASSAGE POINT TO THE GOSPEL?

HOW SHOULD YOU RESPOND TO THIS PASSAGE? WHAT SPECIFIC ACTION STEPS CAN YOU TAKE THIS WEEK TO APPLY THIS PASSAGE?

WRITE A PRAYER OF RESPONSE TO YOUR STUDY OF GOD'S WORD.

Adore God for who He is, confess sins that He revealed in your own life, ask Him to empower you to walk in obedience, and pray for anyone who comes to mind as you study.

WEEK 8 DAY 1

"

IF YOU WANT TO KNOW THE HEART
OF GOD, LOOK TO THE CROSS.

THE GLORY OF THE CROSS

READ: JOHN 13:21-38

CROSS REFERENCE:

Colossians 1:15-20
Hebrews 1:3
Leviticus 19:18
1 John 4:19

In the verses before, Jesus had given His disciples the call again to follow Him, yet the start of today's passage finds Jesus troubled in Spirit. He was troubled because He knew that all of the disciples would not follow Him. One of them would betray Him. Jesus gave a clear sign as to which disciple it was, but the others seemed oblivious to what He was saying. The thought of Jesus being betrayed by one of His own seemed implausible. How could it be?

With Judas having left the others, verse 31 begins Jesus's final discourse to the disciples. He is beginning to say goodbye to them and over the next few chapters will leave them with final words of encouragement and exhortation. The start of this final discourse points us to the glory of the Son and the glory of the Father. As backwards as it seemed to human ears, Jesus wanted them to know that what was about to happen would be the most glorious moment in all of history because it would put God's glory on display. It would point to Jesus as a tangible representation of who God is and His indescribable glory. Jesus is the image of the invisible God, and in Him, the fullness of God was pleased to dwell (Colossians 1:15-20). Jesus Himself is the radiance of the glory of God before our eyes (Hebrews 1:3). For generations, the world longed to know who God is, and with the coming of Jesus, the world could see God.

> Jesus Himself is the radiance of the glory of God before our eyes.

God's glory is who He is, and the cross would put the glorious character of God on display for all to see. The cross would be the single moment in all of human history when God's glory would be most fully revealed. God's perfect plan and the reversal of the curse would be brought to light at the cross. For every person who wants to know who God is, look to Jesus. If you want to know the heart of God, look to the cross. It is at the cross that God's glorious character is revealed. It is at the cross where love, grace, faithfulness, and justice shine forth.

You can hear Jesus pleading with those He loved so dearly. He would not be with them long, and there was so much to tell them. He instructed them that He was giving a new commandment. They were to love one another in the way that He had loved them. This is how the world would know that they were His disciples. At first glance, it does not seem like a new commandment. The commandment to love your neighbor had been seen back in Leviticus 19:18. But the motive and the result of this love was different. They were not commanded to simply love their neighbors but to love as Jesus loved them. They knew that He loved them dearly, and soon they would see that love displayed in the most magnificent way on the cross. This love was humble and sacrificial. It was faithful and infinite. 1 John 4:19 reminds us that we love only because He has loved us first. All of our love flows from His love for us.

The motive of the love was Christ's incomparable love. The result of the love would be that the world would know they were His disciples. This would be the defining mark of Christians—that they love one another. At the time these words were spoken, the world knew who Jesus's disciples were because they followed Him, and they were with Him, but Jesus says that when He is gone, there would be one distinguishing mark that would catch the world's attention. Jesus's disciples are people who love just as Jesus Himself loved.

The passage ends with a short interaction between Jesus and Peter. Peter was fervent. He wanted to be with Jesus. He did not want Jesus to leave. But he also allowed his pride to blind him to his own weakness and sin. Peter could not fathom that he would deny Jesus. Peter did not fully understand that in himself he did not have the strength to resist temptation. There is danger in thinking that we are above even the most egregious sins, and Peter would soon be humbled by the Lord and reminded of his utter dependence on God's sustaining power.

The tone of the book of John is shifting as we begin to dig into this final discourse, and as disciples of Jesus thousands of years later, these words contain encouragement and exhortation for us as well. Jesus's focus on the glory of God begs us to ask the question of how God is glorified in us. How do our lives bring glory to our Savior's name? Jesus calls us to follow Him and lay down our lives and preferences in humble service, and He is glorified when we do. He calls us to love one another, and He is glorified when the world takes notice. He calls us to be aware of our complete dependence on His sustaining grace in our lives. He is glorified in our weakness. He calls us to fix our eyes on the cross and point the world to the glory of the cross, for He is glorified when the cross is lifted high.

DAY 1 QUESTIONS

1. HOW IS THE CROSS BRINGING GLORY TO GOD BACKWARDS FROM THE WORLD'S PERSPECTIVE?

2. WHAT DOES THE CROSS TEACH US ABOUT WHO GOD IS?

3. HOW CAN YOU LIVE THIS WEEK IN A WAY THAT GOD IS GLORIFIED IN YOUR LIFE?

WEEK 8 DAY 2

"

WHEN OUR HEARTS FEEL FAR FROM GOD, WE MUST LOOK TO JESUS.

THE WAY, THE TRUTH, AND THE LIFE

READ: JOHN 14:1-14

CROSS REFERENCE:

Colossians 1:15-20

Hebrews 1:3

It seems fitting that Jesus would begin this passage with an encouragement to His disciples not to let their hearts be troubled. The news of His coming departure, the betrayal by one of His own, and Peter's denial was likely weighing heavy on their hearts. They did not understand what was happening. They had followed Jesus, and they believed Him to be the Messiah, but life was not going as they had planned. Jesus's words broke through the silence and the heaviness with hope for His own. He did not instruct them to have faith without pointing them to the object of that faith. The answer to their anxieties was Jesus.

He did not leave them hopeless but pointed them to the hope that is found in Him. His encouragement to the disciples is for them to believe in God and believe in Him. Trusting Him is what calms our troubled hearts. But Jesus also shifted their focus to the future. Though Jesus was leaving to return to the Father, there would be a day that they would be with Him again. He spoke to them of their future home. His words were not just about a room or a

> Trusting Him is what calms our troubled hearts.

mansion but about the people of God dwelling in the presence of God. Heaven is not primarily about a place but about a person. The supreme glory of heaven is Jesus. So, the people of God do not look forward to streets of gold but the presence of Jesus. This world will never satisfy the longing in the hearts of God's people. The only thing that will satisfy is Him.

Thomas interjected wanting to know the way. Jesus's response is the sixth "I Am" statement and perhaps the most profound statement in Scripture regarding the exclusivity of Jesus. Jesus responds that He is the way, the truth, and the life. Jesus does not simply know the way, tell the truth, and possess life. He is the way, the truth, and the life. And there is no other way than through Him. This statement stands in sharp contrast to the ideologies of our day. Jesus leaves no room for question. Jesus is the only way to God. He is the total embodiment of truth. He is life itself.

Phillip asked Jesus to show them the Father, and Jesus reminded them that they had seen the Father through Him. Jesus is, as we were reminded yesterday, the image of the invisible God, and in Him the fullness of God was pleased to dwell (Colossians 1:15-20). Jesus Himself is the radiance of the glory of God before our eyes (Hebrews 1:3). The triune God was made manifest to humanity through the person of Jesus.

Jesus proclaimed to them that those who believe in Him will do greater things than He did. Certainly, He was not saying that they would somehow be greater than He is but instead that through His power, they would continue His work. The gospel would spread through the work of the disciples after the ascension further than it ever did when Jesus was on Earth. It would go to the ends of the earth, and God would redeem His own from every tribe, tongue, and nation. They would go forth after Jesus was glorified with the message of the cross and the power of the resurrection. The departure of Jesus did not mean the end of His mission but the start of a new chapter of God's people spreading the gospel to all who would hear.

The passage concludes with a promise from Jesus that will be echoed several times in this final discourse. It is the promise of answered prayer. It is the promise that anything asked in the name of Jesus will be given. This promise is not designed to illicit prayers for health, wealth, and happiness. Instead, it is a call to align our hearts to the heart of God. To ask anything in His name is to ask according to God's character and will. And any prayer that is aligned to the heart of God will be answered. The goal of prayer is the glory of God. Jesus tells us that here. Prayer is communion and fellowship with our God, and its end result and our heart's desire should be that God is glorified in our asking and in His answering.

The words of Jesus to the disciples bring hope for us as well. The answer to our anxieties is Jesus. When our hearts feel far from God, we must look to Jesus. Our troubled hearts can trust in His goodness and love. We look forward in hope to the joy of His presence and know that this world is not our home. When life threatens to steal our joy and we are overwhelmed by the difficulties of life, we can fix our gaze on our true home in the presence of our Savior. We can have confidence in Jesus who is the way, the truth, and the life. We can work for His glory, knowing that He will be faithful to spread the gospel through His own. We can run to Him in prayer, seeking to have hearts aligned to His heart. We can be confident that the plan of God will never fail and live every moment of our lives to bring glory to His name.

DAY 2 QUESTIONS

1   WHY DO YOU THINK THE HEARTS OF THE DISCIPLES WERE TROUBLED? WHAT IS TROUBLING YOUR OWN HEART TODAY?

2   HOW DOES THIS PASSAGE BRING COMFORT FOR YOUR OWN TROUBLES, WORRIES, AND ANXIETIES?

3   HOW DO JESUS' WORDS ON PRAYER ENCOURAGE YOU TO GROW YOUR OWN PRAYER LIFE? HOW CAN YOU DO THAT THIS WEEK?

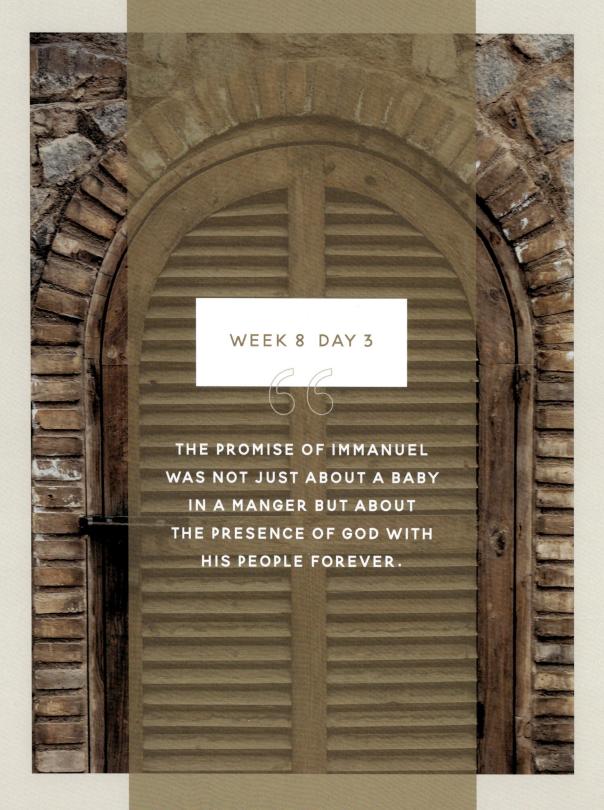

WEEK 8 DAY 3

"

THE PROMISE OF IMMANUEL WAS NOT JUST ABOUT A BABY IN A MANGER BUT ABOUT THE PRESENCE OF GOD WITH HIS PEOPLE FOREVER.

THE PROMISE

READ: JOHN 14:15-31

Things were changing, and change is hard. The disciples were wrestling with all of the changes that Jesus spoke of, and they did not fully understand all that He was telling them. But He did not leave them without hope. To weary and troubled hearts, Jesus offers comfort and peace and the promise of what is to come. Before He encourages their hearts with promises, He reminds them of what He has called them to do.

Those who love Him must keep His commandments. This is what it means to be a disciple. This is what it means to follow Jesus. The people of God are called to obey Him because we love Him. The obedience Jesus was calling the disciples to was not an obedience to gain His love and favor. This was an obedience that flowed out of a deep love for the Savior.

It was true that things were changing, but Jesus would not leave His followers alone. Verse 16 highlights the first mention in Scripture of the Counselor or helper. In Greek, this is the *paraklete*. It

To weary and troubled hearts, Jesus offers comfort and peace.

is most commonly translated as an advocate in Greek literature, but it is a rich word that encompasses many things. Specifically in the biblical text, it also points to this One who comforts, teaches, intercedes, guides, convicts, and empowers. Later in the passage, Jesus will make clear that the *paraklete* is the Holy Spirit. This is the third person of the Trinity. Jesus references the Spirit as another *paraklete* because Jesus is also a *pareklete*. The disciples likely could not imagine what it would be like to not have Jesus by their side, but Jesus assures them that another was coming who would be by their side forever. The Spirit would be with them. He would guide them and teach them, comfort them and sustain them as Jesus had.

Jesus also promised that He would come. He would not leave them alone as orphans. He would come. Verse 20 points out that Jesus would be in them, and they would be in Him. This is union with Christ. Jesus is in His people, and we are in Him. The triune God will come and make His home in His people. Jesus had just told His disciples about His Father's house and their true home that they would go to one day, but now He uses the same imagery and same Greek word to show an extremely significant truth. While the people of God look forward to making a home with God in heaven, in the here and now, God is making His home with us. God dwells with His people. The promise of Immanuel was not just about a baby in a manger but about the presence of God with His people forever.

Finally, Jesus promises peace. Peace was a big topic in the first century world. Shalom was the chosen greeting of the Jewish people at the time, and these words were written during the time period of the Pax Romano or the Peace of Rome. Everyone wanted peace. But the peace Jesus was giving them was unlike any peace the world had ever known. This was His peace. This was peace with God that was made possible through His atoning sacrifice, and it was peace that was not dependent on military victories or political alliances. This peace was His peace and dependent on who He is. This was true shalom. It was wholeness that is found in Jesus alone. They were going to need this peace as they were about to go up against the greatest trial they would ever face as they watched their dearest friend and Savior be crucified. The path ahead of them would be long and hard, with every one of them soon to die a martyr's death in the name of Jesus. Yet through it all, They would cling to His peace. They could go ahead in confidence. Their hearts did not need to be troubled, and they had nothing to fear. They would never be forsaken.

Change is hard, but Jesus is greater. He never leaves us alone. Perhaps you have wondered what it would be like to have Jesus sitting in the same room as you and telling you what to do next in your life. This passage reminds us that the children of God have the Spirit inside them to guide them. We are never apart from His comfort, guidance, intercession, conviction, teaching, and empowerment to serve. The third person of the Trinity is alive in us, and we can live in the power of the Holy Spirit. Jesus reminded the disciples that if they loved Him, they would keep His commandments, and we can be reminded of that same truth. Disciples are marked by obedience and surrender. This is not calling us to a life where we try harder; it is calling us to a life of love. Our obedience should be motivated by our love for Jesus. So, if we find ourselves struggling to obey, the answer to that struggle should not be to try harder but to cultivate our love for Jesus. This is what will motivate us to obedience and surrender. We obey, not in our own strength but through the power of the Spirit in us. We give our lives for the One who gave everything for us.

DAY 3 QUESTIONS

1 HOW DOES LOVE MOTIVATE OBEDIENCE AND SURRENDER?

2 WHAT DOES THIS PASSAGE TEACH US ABOUT THE HOLY SPIRIT?

3 HOW IS THE PEACE THAT JESUS GIVES DIFFERENT THAN THE WORLD'S DEFINITION OF PEACE?

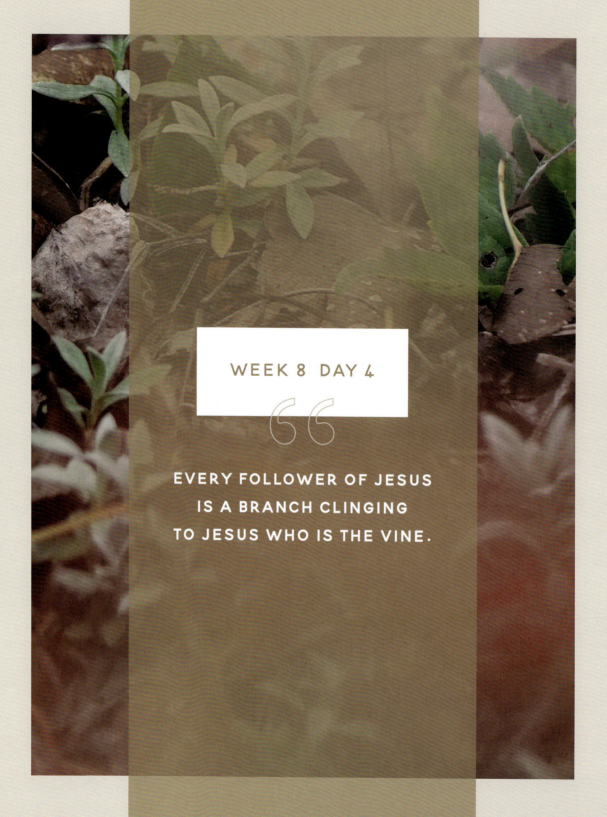

WEEK 8 DAY 4

"

EVERY FOLLOWER OF JESUS IS A BRANCH CLINGING TO JESUS WHO IS THE VINE.

ABIDE

READ: JOHN 15:1-11

CROSS REFERENCE:

John 4:23
John 6:32
John 17:3
Psalm 80:8-19
Isaiah 5:1-7
Jeremiah 2:21
Jeremiah 6:8-9
Ezekiel 17:6-8
Ezekiel 19:10-14
Hosea 10:1-2

John 15 contains some of the most beautiful imagery in Scripture. It is here that Jesus declares that He is the true Vine. It is also here that Jesus declares the final "I Am" statement of the book of John. He presents a picture of a vine and its branches. Jesus is the true Vine. Though there were other vines and other paths, He was the only true Vine. This again is a statement of the exclusivity of Christ. Several other passages in the book of John use the word "true" to make distinctions. The Father is seeking true worshipers (John 4:23), Jesus is the true bread from heaven (John 6:32), and God alone is the true God (John 17:3). Jesus was giving a picture of Himself as the true Vine and the source of all life and sustenance. He was setting a vivid image in the minds of His disciples and all who would read these words of what it means to be a disciple, what it means to live for Jesus, and what it means to live connected to the Vine and source of our life.

The image of the vine is not a new image in Scripture. Throughout the Old Testament, the people of Israel were compared to a vine (Psalm 80:8-19, Isaiah 5:1-7, Jeremiah 2:21, 6:8-9, Ezekiel 17:6-8, 19:10-14, Hosea 10:1-2). This was one of the most prominent images presented in the Old Testament and sets the backdrop for us to understand this passage. Perhaps the most

Though there were other vines and other paths, He was the only true Vine.

prominent of these passages is Isaiah 5. This passage names Israel as the vine and tells the story of Israel through the image of the vine. God had chosen and intentionally planted this vine. He cultivated it and cared for it. He had created them to flourish, but they did not bear good fruit. They yielded wild grapes. The vineyard would be removed because it had failed to bear fruit. Isaiah 5 paints a dismal picture of the vine.

But in John 15, Jesus presents Himself as the true Vine that Israel could never be. He is the true and better Israel. He is the Vine chosen by the Father before the foundations of the world and intentionally planted in the midst of humanity in the fullness of time to redeem His own. He was sent to flourish and redeem. He would do what Israel could never do.

Jesus declares Himself to be the true Vine and then speaks of His own. Every follower of Jesus is a branch clinging to Jesus who is the Vine. Like a branch that is intimately connected to the vine, every child of God is fused to Jesus. The people of God are sustained by this connection. The people of God are also to bear fruit. This is the evidence that a person is redeemed. It is impossible to be a disciple and not bear fruit. And those who do not bear fruit will face judgment.

Growing in godliness is not an easy journey. It will take the careful cultivation of the Lord, and it will involve pruning that is often painful and hard. When the vine is pruned, things are cut away so that the branch can live up to its full potential. In the life of a Christian, this is true as well. The Lord prunes us. He cuts away the things that distract us from the mission He has given us. He allows us to face suffering so that we will learn to trust Him. He disciplines us because He loves us. He cuts away what needs to be cut away so that we can flourish.

So, the Christian is called to a life of abiding. This is remaining and living in light of the connection between us and Christ. It is moment by moment dependence. It is a constant understanding that our lives are meaningless without Him. It is a reminder of our weakness and of His unmatched strength. To abide is to live in light of the gospel, so we must preach the gospel to our hearts each and every day. Apart from Jesus, we are just like the nation of Israel, unable to bear fruit in our own strength. But Jesus has come in our place. He has lived the perfect life we could not live and died the death that we deserved so that we may be connected to Him in an unshakable union. The call of John 15 is a call to stop living in our own strength and to live every moment utterly dependent on who Jesus is and what He has done.

The result of living a life of abiding is the glory of God. Verse 8 tells us that the Father is glorified as we bear much fruit. Glorifying God is the great mission of our lives, and it is accomplished as we are molded and shaped into the image of Christ. It is brought to fruition as we draw life from Jesus and live in His strength. The other result of abiding is joy. As we abide, we experience the joy of Christ in us, and our joy is full and overflowing. Our joy is hinged to Jesus. It is not dependent on anything but Him. As we grow in our relationship with Him, we experience more and more the joy that only He can give.

DAY 4 QUESTIONS

1. HOW DOES ISAIAH 5:1-7 HELP YOU TO UNDERSTAND THIS PASSAGE?

2. READ THROUGH THE PASSAGE AND CIRCLE EVERY TIME THAT THE WORD "ABIDE" IS FOUND.

3. WHAT DOES IT MEAN TO ABIDE? HOW CAN ABIDING BE PRACTICALLY LIVED OUT EACH DAY?

WEEK 8 DAY 5

“

As the people of God have their hearts aligned to the Father's will in prayer, they will pray and desire the will of God above all.

LOVE AND PRAYER

READ: JOHN 15:12-17

CROSS REFERENCE:

Romans 5:8

Ephesians 1:4

Matthew 28:19

Jesus had so much to say to His disciples as He prepared to leave this earth, but there were several things he reminded them over and over again. This passage reminds us of some of those things. Jesus wanted to make sure they knew about their relationship with Him and what He had called them to do. These chapters that included Jesus's final words reiterate some of these key themes multiple times as Jesus leaves His final message for the disciples.

It should be no surprise that Jesus again returns to the theme of love. His commandment to the disciples is that they love one another as they have been loved by Him. In one sense, it sounded like an impossible request. They could not love just like Jesus loved. His love far surpasses any human love, but Jesus asked them to love as He loved, in the same self-sacrificing way. His love was to transform the way that they loved. Just as Jesus had washed the feet of His disciples, they were to humbly serve one another. Just as He would offer Himself as a sacrifice, they should be willing to lay down their preferences for the good of each other. Jesus declared that the greatest love is love that lays down its life for friends. This was not meant to be a pithy phrase about close friendship or even about the sacrificial lives of service men and

> His love was to transform the way that they loved.

women. This was pointing the disciples to the cross. He pointed them to the cross and the atoning sacrifice of Calvary. It was there that He gave everything for those who were yet His enemies (Romans 5:8). It was there that He laid down His life for the ones He came to redeem.

These words also pointed the disciples to their calling as friends of God. Jesus, the Messiah, called them His friends. Though He had spoken the world into existence by the power of His words, and though He knew everything about them, He called them friends. The people of God were so closely knit to the Savior like a branch to a vine that they would share in His mission as friends and co-heirs with Christ. So great was this union that the people of God would share in the glory of the Son and be named as friends. And the evidence of this friendship is obedience and surrender. It is abiding. This is what signals to the world and to our own hearts that we are His.

In verse 16, Jesus reminded them that they did not choose Him. They would have never chosen to follow Him in their own strength. They were lost in their sin and unable to choose to follow Him on their own. But Jesus sought them out. When they were dead in their sins, He made them alive. When they were living lives devoid of purpose, He called them to follow Him. He chose them before the foundations of the world, and the same is true for every child of God (Ephesians 1:4). The people of God are chosen and called by name into a relationship with the God of the world.

His gracious and sovereign choosing comes with a call to action. He has called His own to go and bear fruit. And this fruit is to be fruit that lasts. The words of Jesus to go and bear fruit may bring to mind Jesus's final words to His disciples before He ascended to heaven in Matthew 28:19. In a passage often referred to as the Great Commission, Jesus commands His followers and all who would follow Him to go and make disciples. This is the fruit that lasts and abides. It is the fruit of lives forever changed by the gospel of grace. Jesus shifts their gaze off of the momentary struggles of life and points them to the things that matter for eternity. He ends with a final call to prayer. All that is asked in His name and according to His will, will be given. As the people of God have their hearts aligned to the Father's will in prayer, they will pray and desire the will of God above all.

As the people of God, we are commanded to love one another because we have been loved so greatly. We must stand in awe of the gospel of God's grace that we have been chosen before the foundations of the world, made the friends of God, and now called to abide and find life in His name. We are called to live in light of eternity because today matters for eternity. The way we love, the people we reach, the prayers we pray, and the way we live will have an eternal impact. Jesus calls us to live in light of our union with Him. We are in Him, and He is in us, and that enables us to live every moment for His glory.

DAY 5 QUESTIONS

1 HOW IS JESUS THE PERFECT EXAMPLE OF LOVE?

2 HOW CAN WE LOVE OTHERS AS HE HAS LOVED US?

3 HOW SHOULD ABIDING IN CHRIST CHANGE THE WAY THAT WE LIVE AND PRAY?

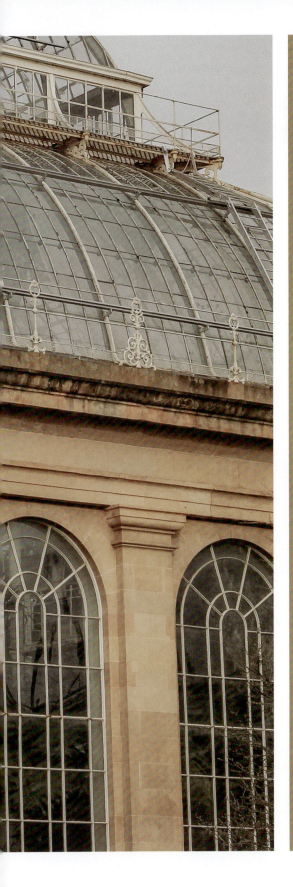

WEEK 8

SCRIPTURE MEMORY

JOHN 1:14

The Word became flesh and dwelt among us. We observed his glory, the glory as the one and only Son from the Father, full of grace and truth.

WEEK EIGHT REFLECTION

REVIEW
John 13:21 – 15:17

PARAPHRASE THE PASSAGE FROM THIS WEEK.

WHAT DID YOU OBSERVE FROM THIS WEEK'S TEXT ABOUT GOD AND HIS CHARACTER?

WHAT DOES THIS WEEK'S PASSAGE REVEAL ABOUT THE CONDITION OF MANKIND AND YOURSELF?

HOW DOES THIS PASSAGE POINT TO THE GOSPEL?

HOW SHOULD YOU RESPOND TO THIS PASSAGE? WHAT SPECIFIC ACTION STEPS CAN YOU TAKE THIS WEEK TO APPLY THIS PASSAGE?

WRITE A PRAYER OF RESPONSE TO YOUR STUDY OF GOD'S WORD.

Adore God for who He is, confess sins that He revealed in your own life, ask Him to empower you to walk in obedience, and pray for anyone who comes to mind as you study.

WEEK 9 DAY 1

> BELIEVERS SHARE IN THE LIFE OF CHRIST, AND PART OF THAT IS SHARING IN HIS SUFFERINGS.

IF THE WORLD HATES YOU

READ: JOHN 15:18-16:4

CROSS REFERENCE:

2 Timothy 3:12

Jesus wanted His disciples to be prepared for everything they would face when He was gone. They were still struggling to process all that was happening and all that He was saying, but He knew they would remember these words long after He had ascended to the Father. So, He encouraged them to abide, and He exhorted them to lives of steadfastness. He warned them that they would face opposition. The people of God are not people of this world, and that brings opposition. As Paul would later warn in 2 Timothy 3:12, all who desire to live godly lives will face persecution. Believers share in the life of Christ, and part of that is sharing in His sufferings.

Jesus reminded the disciples that they were not of the world. They had been chosen out of the world. The world here is not the globe, but it is the world's system of thinking. It is the way of thinking and living that depends on human wisdom, instead of the wisdom of God revealed in Jesus. He urges them to remember His words and remember what He had taught them. They would follow in His footsteps and face the world's hatred

> "The blood of the martyrs is the seed of the church." –Tertullian

just as Jesus did. They would be persecuted because they were His and for the sake of His name. The world's hatred for Jesus and His substitutionary atonement is great. They would crucify Him again if they could, so they persecute His own. Western culture may have different ideas when it comes to persecution. In this culture, the first thought may be of being mocked or left out, but in many places around the world, Christians fear for their lives as they stand for the name of Jesus. Tertullian, an early Christian author, famously said that, "The blood of the martyrs is the seed of the church." This has stood true through the ages. From the time that Christ ascended until the present time, believers have been persecuted and even killed for their faith in Christ, yet the gospel cannot be stopped. The shed blood of the people of God spreads the message of God's love even further. The gospel goes forth in the power of God, and nothing that this world will ever do can stop it.

Jesus's presence had revealed the sinful hearts of those who He encountered. His light shone on the darkness of their sin and revealed them for who they were. Throughout the book of John, we have seen many believe, but there were still many who rejected the gospel message that Jesus brought. They were content to stay in the kingdom of darkness instead of being welcomed into the kingdom of God. Jesus exposed their sin, and they now had no excuse. They hated Him without cause. Though the sinless Son of God had done nothing wrong, He was hated for who He was. Though He had come to rescue and redeem the lost, the weary, and the broken, there were some who hated Him for it.

The news that they would be hated by the world was heavy, but Jesus reminded them of the promised Holy Spirit who would come. He would go with them and guide them. They would not be alone. Chosen in Christ before time began, His disciples would follow Him because they were His. The Spirit would empower them to do what God had called them to do.

Persecution reveals hearts. And it would soon be made clear to those who were true disciples and those who had simply followed the crowd in watching Jesus's miracles. The text says that they would be put out of the synagogues. In this community-based society, this meant that some would lose everything. They would lose their faith communities, their families, their friends, their sources of income, and their homes. Some would give all to follow Christ, and some would even give their lives. Yet Jesus told them that this would lay ahead. These are sobering words spoken to the disciples and sobering words for every child of God to read.

The cost of following Jesus is great, but it is always worth it. Every child of God will face opposition in the name of Jesus, but it is a gift to suffer in His name. We follow in the path of a Savior who suffered to lay down His life for our sin. We walk the path He walked, but we do not do it alone. He was hated, mocked, falsely accused, and rejected. We may be as well. But we are never alone. He is with us, and He has put His Spirit inside us to guide us and strengthen us to do what He has called us to do. We are His, and we have nothing to fear.

DAY 1 QUESTIONS

1. WHY DO YOU THINK THE WORLD HATES THE PEOPLE OF GOD?

2. HOW IS JESUS OUR EXAMPLE OF SUFFERING AND HOW TO FACE PERSECUTION?

3. HAVE YOU EVER FACED PERSECUTION OF ANY KIND FOR BEING A FOLLOWER OF JESUS? HOW CAN THIS GROW YOUR DEPENDENCE ON THE LORD?

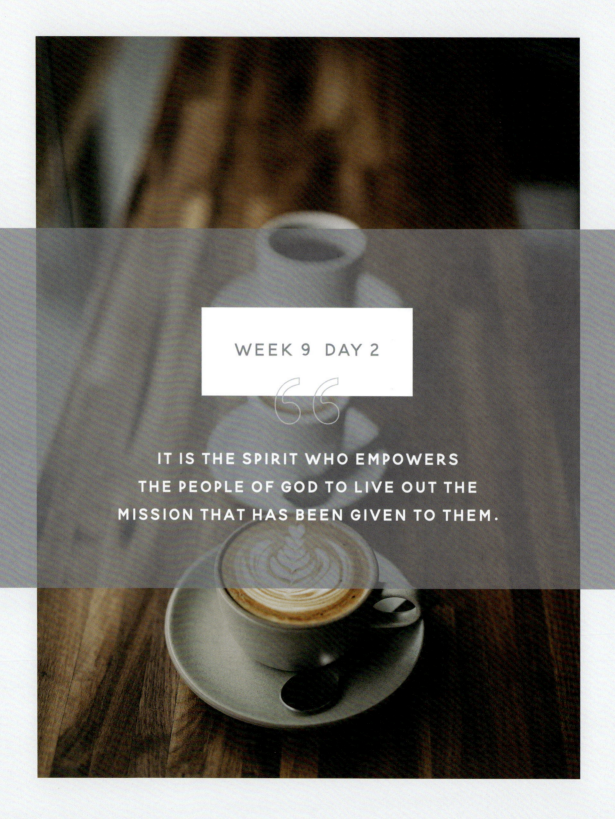

WEEK 9 DAY 2

"

IT IS THE SPIRIT WHO EMPOWERS THE PEOPLE OF GOD TO LIVE OUT THE MISSION THAT HAS BEEN GIVEN TO THEM.

THE SPIRIT AND THE MISSION

READ: JOHN 16:4-15

Everything was changing. And for the disciples it must have felt like their whole world was crumbling and crashing in around them. They had dedicated their lives to Jesus and been ostracized because of it. They had given up everything to follow Him, and now He was leaving. Throughout Jesus's ministry, so many had been confused about who He was and what the Messiah had come to do. The Jews had expected a political leader, but Jesus was so much different than their expectations. The disciples had seen glimpses of the kingdom, but it seems a part of them still hung on to the hope of Jesus as an earthly and political king. Now He was leaving, and they did not know what to do or how to go on. Sorrow mingled with fear, and anxiety gripped their hearts as they looked ahead.

But Jesus brought words of comfort to them. He told them that it was actually a good thing that He leave, because He was sending the Spirit to them. The Holy Spirit is the third person of the Trinity. He is a person. He is fully God and has always been. He is seen throughout the Old Testament but would be seen in this new era in a fuller way. The Spirit would empower the disciples to accomplish the mission that Jesus called them to.

The Spirit is working in ways that humanity cannot fully understand.

The role of the Spirit is significant and transformational in the life of the disciples and in the life of every child of God. The Spirit is no less needed than the Father and the Son. Here and in other passages, Jesus makes clear who the Spirit is and what He does. The Spirit is sent by God to the people of God. It is the Spirit who convicts of sin and the Spirit who regenerates to new life. The Spirit is working in ways that humanity cannot fully understand to draw a lost world to God, and the people of God are invited to join Him in this great mission to bring the kingdom to Earth.

The Spirit is not only active in the work of salvation but also in the daily walk of every believer. The Spirit who inspired the Word of God to the biblical writers also illuminates and gives understanding of the Word of God in the hearts of every believer. The Spirit is our teacher. We do not read the Bible alone but with the guidance of the Spirit who draws our hearts to truth. The Spirit intercedes for us to the Father and prays when we do not even know what to pray. The Spirit is the Comforter as Jesus promised. He provides guidance and counsel, comfort and wisdom. It is the Spirit who sanctifies and grows each child of God in godliness, manifesting the fruit of the Spirit in the lives of believers. It is not our own strength that allows us to grow in grace but the work of the Spirit who is constantly working in our hearts to make us more and more like Jesus. The Spirit changes us.

And it is the Spirit who empowers the people of God to live out the mission that has been given to them. The Spirit is a great gift to every child of God, and as painful as it was for Jesus to depart, He promises to send this great gift to His disciples. The disciples would never be alone. The people of God will never be alone.

As Jesus prepared to leave, He left the disciples with a mission and a promise. Their mission was to proclaim the good news of the gospel to the world, and the promise was that the Spirit would empower them and go with them. These things are true for us today as well. We too are called to this mission to make disciples of all nations. And we too do not go forward in our own strength but in the strength of the Spirit within us. We are never alone, for the Spirit is with us.

DAY 2 QUESTIONS

1   WHAT DO WE LEARN IN THIS PASSAGE ABOUT THE HOLY SPIRIT?

2   WHY DO YOU THINK JESUS SAID THAT IT WAS BETTER FOR HIM TO GO AWAY?

3   HOW CAN YOU WALK IN THE SPIRIT THIS WEEK?

WEEK 9 DAY 3

JESUS CHANGES EVERYTHING. HE REDEEMS EVERYTHING. JESUS REDEEMS OUR PAST, OUR PRESENT, AND OUR FUTURE.

SORROW TO JOY

READ: JOHN 16:16-33

CROSS REFERENCE:

Genesis 3

The time was drawing near. Jesus would soon breath His last breath as He hung on the cross. This news, though not yet fully understood, was weighing on the disciples. They did not understand what was happening. How did this fit into God's plan? Jesus told them that soon they would see Him no longer, but soon after that, they would see Him. He was pointing them to the resurrection. Though all hope would seem lost for three days, the Son of God would raise victorious and return to them. The disciples muttered to one another about the meaning of Jesus's words when Jesus spoke to the questions they were too afraid to ask.

The overarching promise in this passage is that their sorrow would be turned to joy. Jesus did not sugarcoat the truth. Things were hard, and they were about to get even harder, but all was not lost. This was not a hopeless situation. In fact, these days would stand for eternity as a beacon of the only hope of the world. The disciples would weep and lament at the depths of their loss, and the watching world would rejoice in their suffering. Even in death, Jesus would be mocked and derided. There would be sorrow. There would be tears. There would be struggle. But sorrow, tears, and suffering would not last forever. God turns sorrow into joy.

> These days would stand for eternity as a beacon of the only hope of the world.

Jesus pointed them to the natural pattern of a woman giving birth. He refers to her time of delivery and says there will be suffering, but it will not last forever. This suffering is overcome by the joy of new life. The disciples would rightly grieve the loss of their Savior and friend, but that sorrow would not last forever. Because three days later, life would burst forth from a tomb of death. Their sorrow would be replaced by rejoicing, and no one would take this joy from the people of God. The resurrection brings God's people unshakable joy. Nothing can take this joy because Jesus is alive.

Jesus again calls the disciples to prayer and points to prayer as the thing that would increase their joy. Prayer is relationship and communion with God, and it leads to joy. It aligns our hearts with God and teaches us to depend on Him in every moment. Though life would not be easy, Jesus points the disciples to the place where joy is found, and it is always in Him.

The final verses point the disciples to the Father. Jesus declares to them that they will have access to the Father. For those accustomed to the doctrines of Christianity, it could be easy to gloss over this point. This was radical. God's people would no longer have to go through a priest or bring sacrifices. Instead, they would have access to God because of what Jesus had done. From the first pages of Genesis, the Bible tells a story of a world broken by sin and living under the imminent defeat of death. But Jesus reverses the story. He changes the narrative. Jesus heals the brokenness that sin had caused, and Jesus defeats the power of death. The communion with God that was broken in Genesis 3 is restored through the work of Christ. It is interesting to note that as Jesus speaks of the incarnation, He uses the Greek perfect tense. He speaks of a past that has present and future implications. Jesus changes everything. He redeems everything. Jesus redeems our past, our present, and our future.

Jesus finishes this discourse with the truth that He has said these things to give them peace. It would be a tumultuous journey ahead, but the Word of God would be the bedrock of their faith and the source of their peace. Jesus's promise to them that is true for all believers is that in the world there will be tribulation. This is what we are called to—to walk in the path of a persecuted Savior. We are called to bear shame, rejection, and contempt in His name. But there is overflowing hope for the people of God and unshakable joy. Jesus is no longer in the grave. He has overcome the world.

There are times when we do not feel the victory of the cross. Instead, we feel the weight of life in a broken world. What a sweet reminder it is that Jesus spoke these words declaring how He had overcome before the cross and the resurrection took place. It had not happened yet, but it was as certain as the past. The people of God can look back to the cross, even in a world of brokenness, and know that Jesus has overcome the world. We can take heart, because the victory is won. We can look ahead in faith, knowing that Jesus is coming back. He will bring the consummation of this world and implant in our hearts unshakable joy and overflowing peace.

DAY 3 QUESTIONS

1. HOW DOES GOD TURN OUR SORROW INTO JOY?

2. HOW DOES THE WORD OF GOD BRING US PEACE?

3. PARAPHRASE AND APPLY JOHN 16:33.

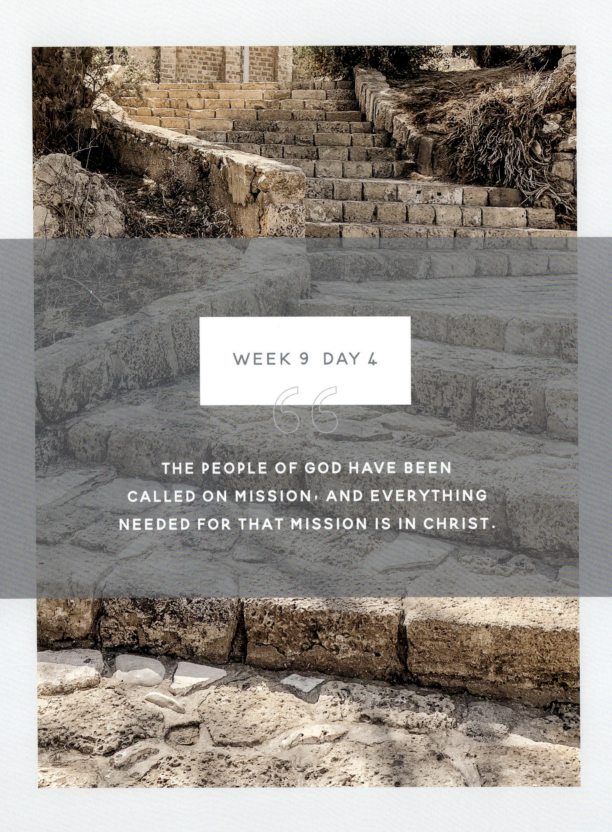

WEEK 9 DAY 4

"

THE PEOPLE OF GOD HAVE BEEN CALLED ON MISSION, AND EVERYTHING NEEDED FOR THAT MISSION IS IN CHRIST.

THE PRAYER OF JESUS

READ: JOHN 17:1-26

CROSS REFERENCE:

Exodus 34:5-7

1 John 3:2

John 17 is one of the most beautiful passages in Scripture because it gives us such incredible insight into who Jesus is, His love for His people, and the mission to which He has called them. This passage is known as the High Priestly Prayer since very early days of church history. Some have also referred to it as Jesus's consecration prayer and the Lord's Prayer. With Jesus's final discourse finished, he turns to heaven and prays to the Father as the crucifixion approaches. Verse 1 contains the seventh and final mention of Jesus's hour. His hour has come, and His response is to turn to the Father in prayer.

The prayer is stunningly focused on the glory of God. Believers today can be moved by the love of Christ for us but also encouraged to pray and live for the glory of God as Jesus demonstrated to us. The glory of the Son and the glory of the Father are the subject of the start of the prayer, and we see that this glory is intrinsically connected to the cross. The glory of God is manifested fully at the cross. This is the moment that all of history has been groaning for since the fall. This is what history has been moving toward since the dawn of creation. This is the plan of God, formed before time ever began. Jesus accomplished the work that He had come to do, and it would soon be declared as finished. Jesus had come to save and fulfill His covenant of redemption, and He would accomplish what He had come to do.

> His hour has come, and His response is to turn to the Father in prayer.

The Gospel of John has placed a great emphasis on the glory of Jesus. In the prologue, John described Jesus and declared we have seen His glory. Every moment of Jesus's earthly life and ministry pointed the world to His glory, every anguish-filled moment on the cross displayed His glory, and the empty tomb declared with power the glory of God displayed in Jesus for all the world to see. The glory that the triune God shared before the world existed was being displayed. The book of John opened with a reminder that the Word was with God and was God from the beginning, and now we are seeing the dawn of a new creation as the glory of God is brought to earth as never before.

Jesus had accomplished His mission of redemption, and He had accomplished His mission of manifesting who God is to the world. Jesus reveals to humanity who God is. Moses had begged in Exodus 34:5-7 for just a glimpse of God's glory, and He was told of God's mercy, grace, steadfast love, and faithfulness. The glory of God is who He is. The incarnation of Jesus revealed those eternal truths in a visible way. And the cross was the pinnacle of that revelation. The cross displays all of the attributes of God to the world.

Jesus prayed for Himself and for the glory of God to be manifested, and then He prayed for His disciples and the church. We could likely spend ten weeks just on this prayer. Jesus prays for His chosen people, given to Him by God, the One who initiates salvation. He prays for them as they live in a world that is not their home. He declares the truth that not a single one of God's own will be lost. He prays for their joy to be rooted in Him. He does not ask for them to be removed from this world that will hate and persecute them but for God to guard them from the enemy. The people of God have been called on mission, and everything needed for that mission is in Christ.

Verse 17 tells of the source of the sanctification and growth of God's people, and it is the Word of God. The truth of God will grow and mature all disciples, and Scripture is the truth. The Word that would be written on the pages of Scripture would be the treasure of the people of God to fix their eyes on the Word incarnate that was yet before their eyes. The living Word of God has the power to transform the life of every child of God through the illumination of the Spirit.

Jesus's final prayer is for unity among His Church. The unity displayed in the Trinity for all of eternity would now be embodied in the Church. This would not be a uniformity in which every Christian would be identical but a unity in the midst of diversity. The people of God would be called out from every nation, race, ethic group, language, and period of time, to be unified in Christ. The prayer ends with a reminder of God's love for the Son who is in us as well. These are the marks of the Church. We should be united to Christ and in unity with one another. And as we are loved by God, we should love one another. Jesus's desire for His own is that they see God's glory. One day, we will see Him as He is (1 John 3:2), and for now we see His glory through His Word and the Spirit He has given to guide us. We taste heaven through unity with the Lord and His people.

What a comfort to know that we are His. What an encouragement to live for the glory of God. What an exhortation to build our lives on the Word of God and grow in grace and truth in the likeness of Christ.

DAY 4 QUESTIONS

1 WHAT DO YOU LEARN ABOUT JESUS FROM THIS PRAYER?

2 HOW DOES THE CROSS REVEAL THE CHARACTER AND ATTRIBUTES OF GOD? RECORD SOME SPECIFIC ATTRIBUTES THAT ARE DISPLAYED THROUGH JESUS.

3 HOW CAN YOU APPLY THIS PRAYER? HOW DOES IT CALL YOU TO LIVE? HOW ARE YOU CALLED TO CHANGE? HOW ARE YOU ENCOURAGED?

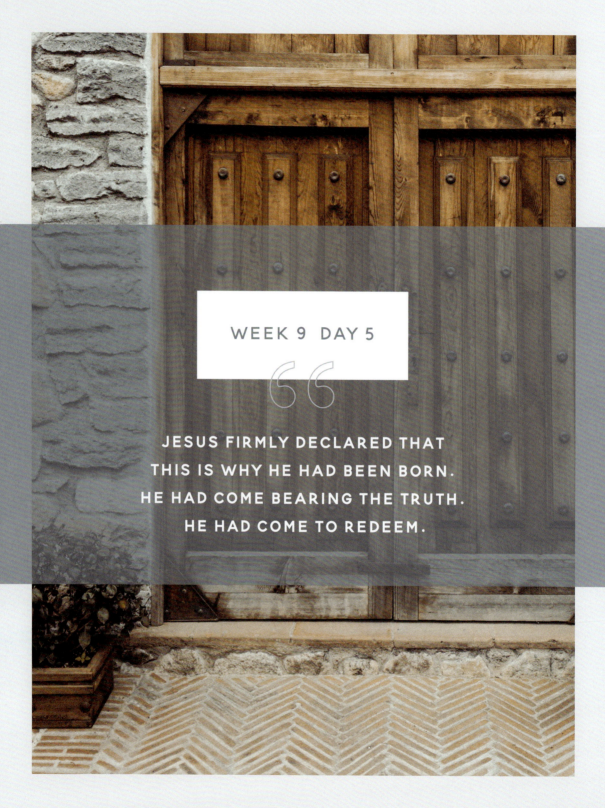

WEEK 9 DAY 5

"

JESUS FIRMLY DECLARED THAT
THIS IS WHY HE HAD BEEN BORN.
HE HAD COME BEARING THE TRUTH.
HE HAD COME TO REDEEM.

THE LAMB ON TRIAL

READ: JOHN 18:1-40

The time has come. The Savior of the world would soon lay down His life. But first, He would be betrayed and arrested. He would be accused and beaten. Jesus had just prayed His high priestly prayer. He had interceded for His own, and He had magnified and glorified the Father. His time of glorification was drawing near, but first would be His humiliation.

This chapter picks up in the garden of Gethsemane. John tells us that it is a place where He met with His disciples often. It must have been a place they had come regularly to pray and fellowship with one another. Since it was a place they had gone often, it would not have seemed unusual to the disciples to go there with Jesus, and it also did not make it difficult for Judas, the betrayer, to find Jesus. The text tells us that Judas brought with him a band of soldiers and religious leaders. With torches in hand, they marched into the garden with a plan to extinguish the Light of the world.

Jesus was there to do the will of the Father.

Jesus did not run or hide. Instead, He offered up Himself. Yet when Jesus said, "I am he," there was no question that He was again claiming to be the I AM. Perhaps the soldiers saw just a glimpse of His glory as they fell to the ground. It was a stunning picture of the fact that His life would not be taken from Him but laid down for the sin of His people. It all must have seemed so out of control for the disciples who were watching. Their whole world was spinning out of control and collapsing around them. Despite all that Jesus had told them about what was ahead, they did not feel prepared for this decisive moment. This is seen so clearly as Peter cuts off the ear of one of the soldiers. He did not want to see this happen. He was likely scared and confused, but Jesus reminded Him that this is why He had come. Jesus was there to do the will of the Father. He would drink the cup that was set before Him. The cup in the Old Testament was a reference to God's holy wrath and judgment, and it would soon be poured out on Jesus in fullest measure.

It is interesting to note that all of this takes place in a garden. Scripture begins and ends with a garden and here finds its pivotal moment in a garden as well. The garden of Gethsemane was necessary because of the fall that took place in the garden of Eden. It was in Eden that Adam fell as the representative of all mankind, and it was here in Gethsemane that Jesus would rise above temptation victoriously for His own. In the garden of Eden, God came looking for the man and woman who were hiding because of their sin. Here in Gethsemane, it seems that man is coming to look for God to put Him to death. Yet even here, it is God who is pursuing. The thoughts and plans of evil men were seeking to kill, but their plans would be used by God to redeem the world.

They arrested Him and bound Him. They paraded Him in front of the high priest. What a shocking picture to see this corrupt high priest accusing the true and better High Priest. It was this same Caiaphas who had devised a plan to put Jesus to death for the sake of the people. From Caiaphas's perspective, this was necessary to make sure the people did not revolt against the established religious and political system. He had no idea how prophetic his words were. Caiaphas's evil plan was part of God's sovereign plan.

In the midst of Jesus's questioning from the high priest, the scene shifts to Peter. The zealous and fervent Peter, who had cut off the ear of a soldier and promised to never forsake Jesus, was having his faith tested. Would he identify with Jesus when things were looking bad? Would he have the courage to name himself as a disciple of Jesus? Sadly, the text records for us three instances of failure in Peter's life. Repeatedly, he denied Jesus. Peter was revealing his deep need for Jesus. He did not have strength on his own to proclaim the hope that is found in Jesus alone. The betrayal must have wounded Jesus deeply. He was being accused and betrayed at the hands of many evil men, but this was different. This was one of His closest friends. Being fully God and fully man, Jesus knew Peter would deny Him yet also felt the bitter sting of rejection. But this would not be the end of Peter's story.

The chapter ends with Jesus going before Pilate. The Jews would not even step foot inside Pilate's home. Jewish tradition stated that it would have defiled them to go into the home of a Gentile. The Passover was near, and they did not want to be unable to participate in the Passover feast. Yet, all the while they were there, seeking to consume the Lamb of God, and the true Passover Lamb.

Pilate interrogated Jesus. He was looking for some crime for which to condemn Him. Jesus stood fast. He humbly declared who He was as the King of a kingdom that was not of this world. In the midst of some of the darkest hours of the crucifixion week, Jesus firmly declared that this is why He had been born. He had come bearing the truth. He had come to redeem. Pilate tried to offer a way out with the offer of setting Jesus free, but the crowd chose Barabbas. The Son of God would be put to death.

Through every horrific moment, God was not taken off guard. God's will would be accomplished through the most painful of circumstances. The details of this story draw our hearts to greater adoration for our Savior and what He endured in our place. But they also give us hope that God is never caught off guard. He uses everything for His glory and our good. And in our own lives, we can rest in this truth. God will be faithful to use the most agonizing moments to bring about His sovereign plan.

DAY 5 QUESTIONS

1 CONSIDER THE SCENE. WHAT DO YOU THINK THE DISCIPLES WOULD HAVE BEEN THINKING AND FEELING? WHAT DO WE OBSERVE ABOUT JESUS FROM THIS PASSAGE?

2 IN WHAT WAYS DOES THIS PASSAGE SHOW US THAT JESUS LAID DOWN HIS LIFE WILLINGLY?

3 GOD WAS NOT CAUGHT OFF GUARD BY THE EVENTS THAT SURROUNDED THE CRUCIFIXION. HOW DOES THAT ENCOURAGE YOU IN YOUR OWN LIFE?

WEEK 9

SCRIPTURE MEMORY

JOHN 1:15-16

John testified concerning him and exclaimed, "This was the one of whom I said, 'The one coming after me ranks ahead of me, because he existed before me.'" Indeed, we have all received grace upon grace from his fullness

WEEK NINE REFLECTION

REVIEW
John 15:18 – 18:40

PARAPHRASE THE PASSAGE FROM THIS WEEK.

WHAT DID YOU OBSERVE FROM THIS WEEK'S TEXT ABOUT GOD AND HIS CHARACTER?

WHAT DOES THIS WEEK'S PASSAGE REVEAL ABOUT THE CONDITION OF MANKIND AND YOURSELF?

HOW DOES THIS PASSAGE POINT TO THE GOSPEL?

HOW SHOULD YOU RESPOND TO THIS PASSAGE? WHAT SPECIFIC ACTION STEPS CAN YOU TAKE THIS WEEK TO APPLY THIS PASSAGE?

WRITE A PRAYER OF RESPONSE TO YOUR STUDY OF GOD'S WORD.

Adore God for who He is, confess sins that He revealed in your own life, ask Him to empower you to walk in obedience, and pray for anyone who comes to mind as you study.

WEEK 10 DAY 1

"

THE CROSS REMINDS US WHO GOD IS. IT TELLS OF HIS HOLINESS, JUSTICE, WRATH, MERCY, GRACE, LOVE, AND SO MUCH MORE.

THE DEATH OF THE KING

READ: JOHN 19:1-42

CROSS REFERENCE:

Acts 2:23-24

Leviticus 16:27

Hebrews 13:13

Psalm 34:20

Psalm 22:18

Zechariah 12:10

Isaiah 53

Hebrews 12:2-3

The cross is the center of Christianity, and it is in this beautiful chapter that we see the anguish and glory of the cross. Jesus was beaten and bloody. He was given a sham of a trial and condemned by those He came to save. He could have called angels to rescue Him. He could have rescued Himself, but instead He humbly submitted Himself to the most cruel and humiliating death to ransom His own.

In the wake of torture and humiliation, Pilate prodded Jesus and declared his own authority. Jesus's answer is a powerful and telling reminder that through it all, man was never in control. The only authority that Pilate had was the authority that had been given to him by God. Lawless and sinful men had merely carried out the sovereign plan of God (Acts 2:23-24). The evil of this world had no power to stop the sovereign plan of God. Jesus was beaten and bruised. He was tortured and abused, but He did it willingly in our place. His life was not taken from Him but given willingly.

The evil of this world had no power to stop the sovereign plan of God.

Pilate tried to shift the blame as humans often do. As He called Jesus the King of the Jews, the crowds roared with hatred and disdain. They said they had no king but Caesar. These people who hated Caesar showed they hated Jesus so much more. They were more willing to bow their knee to the one who had oppressed them, than to Jesus who had come to deliver them. They were blinded by their sin and could not see what was happening before their eyes.

John is careful to note what took place so that the Scriptures would be fulfilled. A close look at this account reveals so many fulfillments of Old Testament prophecies and types. Every part of Scripture points to Jesus, and John makes this abundantly clear. Jesus suffered outside the city at the place where sacrifices were taken under Jewish law, and as an example to us of how we should bear reproach for the name of Jesus (Leviticus 16:27, Hebrews 13:13). And just as Isaac carried the wood for sacrifice up the mountain so long ago and clung to the promise that God would provide Himself a lamb, Jesus, the Lamb of God, carried His cross up that mountain. His bones would not be broken, lots would be cast for His garments, and He would be pierced for our transgressions (Psalm 34:20, 22:18, Zechariah 12:10, Isaiah 53). Every prophecy would be fulfilled so that we might believe.

The words of this chapter can also remind us of many of the events in the opening scenes of Scripture. It was a tree that ushered in the original sin of mankind, and it would be on a tree that the power of sin would be forever broken. It was a serpent that deceived, but here that serpent would be crushed. Adam and Eve's sin in the garden brought with it the shame of nakedness, but here at Calvary, Jesus hung naked and bore our sin and shame. And just as God clothed Adam and Eve in the garden, it is here at the cross that the people of God are clothed in the righteousness of God.

The One who is the living water cried out in thirst before He gave up His life. Yet His cry of thirst from the old rugged cross is a call for all to freely come to Him and drink the living water that only He provides. Then He cried, "It is finished," and Jesus died. The Greek *tetelestai* was commonly stamped on an invoice to signify that it had been paid in full. This single word declared that salvation had been accomplished. Jesus had done what He had come to do and accomplished the Father's will. Jesus had revealed the character of God in His sinless life and here at the cross where all of God's attributes were displayed. He had paid the price of the redemption of His own. He had defeated Satan and crushed death forever.

Jesus suffered in our place. This cannot be overstated. He bore the pain of physical suffering and identified with those who face sickness and chronic pain and illness. He bore the weight of humiliation and shame, identifying with those who feel crushed by shame. He was abused and mocked, identifying with those who have been abused for the sinful gain or pleasure of another. He faced deep emotional and mental anguish, identifying with those who are wearied by such struggles. At the cross, Jesus paid the price of our redemption, but He also identified with us in our suffering. He proved that no matter what we face, we are never alone. And Hebrews 12:2-3 reminds us to look to Jesus and all He has faced and to take heart and not grow weary. We are not alone.

The cross reminds us who God is. It tells of His holiness, justice, wrath, mercy, grace, love, and so much more. The cross reminds us that God is in control. He is not caught off guard by the worst possible circumstances but works all things together for the good of His people and the glory of His great name. The cross reminds us that we are not alone in our suffering. Jesus has suffered in our place, and because of who He is and how He is with us, we know that we are not alone in anything that we face. He sympathizes with us. The cross reminds us to trust the God who has loved us and called us by name.

DAY 1 QUESTIONS

1. AS YOU READ SLOWLY THROUGH THIS PASSAGE, WHAT STANDS OUT TO YOU?

2. WHAT DOES THE CROSS TEACH YOU ABOUT WHO GOD IS?

3. WHAT ENCOURAGEMENT DO YOU FIND IN THE CROSS?

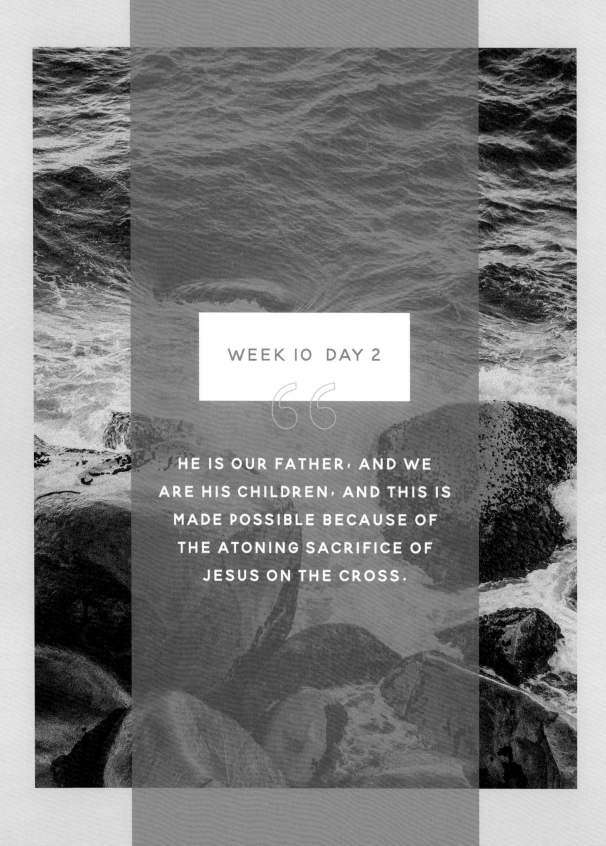

WEEK 10 DAY 2

> HE IS OUR FATHER, AND WE ARE HIS CHILDREN, AND THIS IS MADE POSSIBLE BECAUSE OF THE ATONING SACRIFICE OF JESUS ON THE CROSS.

I HAVE SEEN THE LORD

READ: JOHN 20:1-18

CROSS REFERENCE:

John 10:3-4

Hope must have seemed totally lost. Jesus was buried in a cold tomb, and the disciples now somehow needed to learn to pick up the pieces. The men and women who followed Jesus had dedicated their entire lives to Him, and they must have felt crushed and confused by Jesus's death. Mary was worried that the tomb had been robbed, but it was death that had been robbed that morning by the power of the resurrection.

Mary Magdalene is a prominent figure in the Gospels. She was present at the cross when so many had fled, and now we see her on the first day of the week coming to the tomb early in the morning. She likely came weeping and overwhelmed with grief, but when she got to the tomb, the stone had been rolled away. She ran and brought Peter and John to help her make sense of the empty tomb. Peter and John ran to find the tomb empty just as Mary had said. Lying inside the tomb were the empty grave clothes that sat folded in place. We are told that John believed when He saw the empty tomb. It seems that Jesus's teaching on resurrection was beginning to come together in his mind. Peter and John went home, but Mary stayed.

> He was no longer dead.
> He was risen indeed.

She stood there, weeping outside the tomb and gazing inside when two angels appeared to her and asked her why she was crying. She turned around and saw Him, but she did not even recognize Him at first. She pleaded with Jesus, thinking that perhaps He was the gardener and perhaps He was even the one who had taken the body of Jesus. But then He called her name. In John 10:3-4, Jesus had declared that His sheep know His voice, and here we can observe that in action. Mary recognized His voice as He said her name. Her teacher, her friend, and her Lord stood before her. He was no longer dead. He was risen indeed.

Jesus told her that He would soon be ascending, and His description of what would happen reveals just how much the cross of Christ had accomplished for His people. Over a hundred times throughout the book of John, Jesus had referred to God as Father. In all of these times, God was referred to by Jesus as My Father or the Father. But in light of the resurrection, we see the glorious hope of adoption and restored relationship with the Father. Jesus speaks here of Jesus as "my Father" and "your Father." This is the only time in the Gospel that such a personal pronoun is used to describe the relationship of the Father with anyone but Jesus. This is what the cross of Christ secures for all who believe. It makes them sons and daughters of God. It makes them co-heirs with Christ. The Father and almighty God is not far off; He is near to His children. He is our Father, and we are His children, and this is made possible because of the atoning sacrifice of Jesus on the cross. He is our Father. He is near and personal. He is our God. He is transcendent, high, and holy. Through the blood of Jesus, we who were once far off are brought near to God.

Jesus commanded Mary to go and tell His brothers, the disciples, the news of His resurrection. Because of this Mary has often been referred to as the apostle to the apostles. She proclaimed the good news of the gospel to those who would then proclaim to all the world the news of the risen Savior. She was the first eyewitness of the risen Christ. This is particularly noteworthy because in this first century culture, a woman's testimony was not even admissible in court. In a world that degraded women and regulated them to the sidelines, Jesus elevated them and brought them in. Mary was given the high honor of proclaiming the greatest news of all time: He is risen.

The message that she proclaimed was immensely personal. She had seen the Lord. Though she went to the tomb seeking to weep over His body, she had seen the Lord. She had seen Jesus. She proclaimed the words of the Lord to the disciples and the message that Jesus was alive.

For all those who have placed their faith in the saving work of Jesus, we can say that He is our God. We can call God our Father. Jesus has done what we could never do for ourselves. He has conquered death and defeated the grave. May the testimony of our lips and our lives be the words of Mary: "I have seen the Lord." May our lives be poured out as an offering for the One who has conquered the grave and conquered our hearts.

DAY 2 QUESTIONS

1. WHAT EMOTIONS DO YOU THINK MARY, PETER, AND JOHN WOULD HAVE BEEN FEELING AS THE CAME AND FOUND THE EMPTY TOMB?

2. HOW DOES JESUS' WORK ON THE CROSS CHANGE OUR RELATIONSHIP WITH GOD?

3. HOW HAVE YOU SEEN THE LORD IN YOUR OWN LIFE?

WEEK 10 DAY 3

"

THE CHURCH IS CALLED TO BE A COMMUNITY OF SENT ONES LIVING ON THIS EARTH TO PROCLAIM THE GOSPEL.

LIFE IN HIS NAME

READ: JOHN 20:19-31

On the evening of that resurrection Sunday, Jesus appeared to the disciples just as He had appeared to Mary. He appeared in a room with the doors still locked, and the disciples were left in awe. These men had been grief-stricken and cowering in fear, now fixed their gaze on their resurrected Savior and friend. He came to them and stood in their midst. He declared to them tidings of peace and showed them the wounds on His body. The disciples were filled with peace and joy. The resurrection had changed everything.

But Jesus also came to remind them of the mission that had been assigned to them. The resurrection had changed everything, and now they must go forth and proclaim the message of the gospel to all who would hear. Just as the Father had sent Jesus into the world, the people of God are sent into the world to point the world to Christ. The Church is called to be a community of sent ones living on this earth to proclaim the gospel. He breathed on them the Holy Spirit and encouraged them to preach the gospel.

The resurrection had changed everything.

Verse 23 is easily confusing; however, it is not teaching that the disciples had power to grant forgiveness or damnation. Instead, it is showing the power of the preaching of God's Word. The living and active Word of God would go forth through the disciples and proclaim the gospel message of what only God can do.

The passage then shifts to Thomas. Thomas reveals the struggle of unbelief. And though he has often been called "doubting Thomas," he reveals the seeds of unbelief that easily take root inside every one of us. Thomas wanted to see with his eyes the evidence of the resurrection, and Jesus met him in his unbelief. Jesus came to him to reveal Himself. He did not shame him or push him away. He drew near. Thomas's response was to recognize Jesus as his Lord and God. This is who Jesus is. He is God in flesh, and He is the sovereign Lord. Thomas doubted, but his doubt was transformed into faith by Jesus. Jesus declared blessing on all those who believe without seeing, and yet in many ways, believers throughout the ages have also seen the proof of the resurrected Jesus. We have not seen the scars in His hands and feet, but we have been eye-witnesses to the power of the gospel. We have seen the goodness of God and experienced the power of the Spirit in us. Those who are His children can boldly say that we have seen Him work and know Him intimately.

The chapter ends with the purpose statement of the entire book of John. The words of this chapter, but more so the words of this entire Gospel, are written to produce faith in Jesus Christ. They are written to declare the miracles and signs that point to who He is. They are written to draw our minds to the prophecies of the Old Testament that Jesus perfectly fulfills. They are written to show us the heart of God gloriously displayed in the person of Jesus. They are written so that we might believe. They are written for those who have not yet believed, and they are written for all who have already believed. The book of John is a reminder that Jesus is the only place that life is found.

John says that life is found in believing in His name. Life is found in Jesus alone. This is resurrection life, and it is abundant life. Throughout the Gospel, John has proclaimed that Jesus is where life is. He is the Word of God made flesh. He is the living water that satisfies. He is the bread and the wine. He is the great I AM and the resurrection and the life. He is the Good Shepherd. He is the door and the true Vine. He is the way, the truth, and the life.

Jesus is our life. This is what we must remember as we look to the Gospel of John. Our hope is found in Him, and because of His life, death, and resurrection, we are sent forth as a Church on mission to spread the gospel to the world. He has given us His Holy Spirit to empower and equip us to serve Him. He has promised to go with us. So, we like Thomas can look to Jesus and say, "My Lord and my God." Nothing but Jesus will ever satisfy. Abundant life is found only in Him. We have seen Him, and our lives will never be the same.

DAY 3 QUESTIONS

1. WHAT DO YOU LEARN ABOUT JESUS FROM THE WAY THAT HE INTERACTS WITH THOMAS?

2. WHAT DOES IT MEAN THAT LIFE IS FOUND IN JESUS' NAME?

3. WHAT ARE THE THINGS THAT THIS WORLD SAYS ARE MORE IMPORTANT THAN JESUS TO HAVE A FULFILLED LIFE? HOW IS JESUS BETTER?

WEEK 10 DAY 4

❝

WE LOOK TO JESUS WHO IS OUR LIFE AND HEAR HIM SAY, "FOLLOW ME."

FOLLOW ME

READ: JOHN 21:1-25

CROSS REFERENCE:

1 Peter 2:2-3

The final chapter of the book of John finds the disciples once again on the Sea of Galilee. These fishermen by trade had returned to their hometown and gone out for a catch while they waited for Jesus to instruct them on what was next. Jesus revealed Himself to them once more and gave them a powerful lesson on what it means to live in the strength of the Lord. They had been out all night fishing and had caught nothing. For professional fishermen, this was distressing. But then it happened. Just as the light of dawn began to peek over the horizon, there was a man standing on the shore. His voice called to them asking if they had caught anything, though He already knew what their reply would be. He instructed them to cast their nets on the other side of the boat. Immediately, they obeyed and brought in more fish than they could even bring aboard.

Jesus had made them fishers of men, and the abundant harvest of fish before them was a small glimpse into what the future held for these men of Galilee. The harvest they would reap was abundant. It was more than they could have ever imagined, and it was made possible because of the power of the Lord and His Spirit inside of them.

The harvest they would reap was abundant.

Though they were not sure who the man was up until that point, John looked at Peter and said that it was Jesus. Without hesitating, Peter jumped out of the boat and swam to shore. Peter had just sinned so grievously, but knowing that Jesus was near, he simply wanted to be in His presence. The rest of the disciples came soon after, and Jesus invited them to breakfast. In first century culture, this invitation was a sign of a deep and intimate relationship. Jesus wanted to fellowship with His disciples, and surely this would be a moment that they would never forget.

This sweet time of fellowship was not without difficulty. Peter was painfully aware of his own failure and feeling the shame of sin and regret. But sin needs to be dealt with, and Jesus graciously pressed in. The smell of the campfire reminded Peter of the last time he had been around a fire and how he had denied Jesus three times. And just as Peter had denied the Lord three times, Jesus had three questions for Peter. "Do you love me?" Jesus asked. Peter surely felt the embarrassment of the moment and the weight of his own failure, but Jesus continued to ask the question. Peter's response to the question was yes, and Jesus gave him a commission to feed the sheep.

Peter was not simply being forgiven, but he was being restored. Despite his weakness, God would use Peter greatly to spread the message of the gospel through the entire world. In fact, a look at the books of Acts and 1 and 2 Peter shows a Peter who is humble and bold. The one who had once denied Jesus would be strengthened to do the work of the Lord. He would shepherd the people of God just like Jesus had asked him to do. Peter would later speak of the Word of God as the spiritual food of God's people (1 Peter 2:2-3). And he would preach that Word powerfully and see thousands come to Christ.

Jesus called His disciples to follow Him just as He had at the very beginning. And John, the beloved disciple, ends the book with a sweet reminder that there was so much more that Jesus did while He was here on earth. The world could not contain all the books that could be written of all that Jesus had done and everything that He is. With such beautiful and poetic words, the book of John closes, yet the impact of the gospel story continues to this day.

Just as Jesus called His disciples so long ago, He calls us today. He calls us to turn to Him in faith. He calls us to follow Him with our lives. He calls us to carry our cross and live like Jesus. He reminds us that He has lived the perfect life that we could not live and died the death that we deserved in our place. His grace flows from Calvary for sinners. So, we look to Jesus. We look to the fulfillment of every promise wrapped in the Word become flesh. We look to the cross where He took our sin, guilt, and shame, and clothed us in His perfect righteousness. We look to Jesus who is our life and hear Him say, "Follow Me."

DAY 4 QUESTIONS

1 WHAT DOES THIS PASSAGE TEACH YOU ABOUT RELYING ON GOD'S STRENGTH?

2 HOW DOES PETER'S STORY BRING YOU COMFORT?

3 WHAT DOES THIS PASSAGE TEACH YOU ABOUT JESUS?

WEEK 10 DAY 5

"

- A REVIEW OF JOHN -

Look back through the book of John as you reflect on your time studying this book, and answer the following questions:

1 WHAT STOOD OUT TO YOU MOST IN THE BOOK OF JOHN?

2 IS THERE SOMETHING NEW THAT YOU LEARNED?

3 THINK ABOUT WHAT THE BOOK OF JOHN TEACHES ABOUT WHO JESUS IS. IN JUST A FEW SENTENCES, DESCRIBE WHO JESUS IS.

4 AFTER READING THE BOOK OF JOHN, WHAT ARE YOU MOST THANKFUL FOR?

5 WHAT HAVE YOU LEARNED THAT GOD IS PROMPTING YOU TO APPLY TO YOUR LIFE?

6 WRITE OUT A FINAL PRAYER AS YOU CLOSE THIS STUDY, THANKING GOD FOR WHO HE IS AND ALL THAT HE HAS DONE.

OTHER NOTES AND FAVORITE VERSES FROM JOHN:

WEEK 10

SCRIPTURE MEMORY

JOHN 1:17-18

for the law was given through Moses; grace and truth came through Jesus Christ. No one has ever seen God. The one and only Son, who is himself God and is at the Father's side—he has revealed him.

WEEK TEN REFLECTION

REVIEW
John 19:1 – 21:25

PARAPHRASE THE PASSAGE FROM THIS WEEK.

WHAT DID YOU OBSERVE FROM THIS WEEK'S TEXT ABOUT GOD AND HIS CHARACTER?

WHAT DOES THIS WEEK'S PASSAGE REVEAL ABOUT THE CONDITION OF MANKIND AND YOURSELF?

HOW DOES THIS PASSAGE POINT TO THE GOSPEL?

HOW SHOULD YOU RESPOND TO THIS PASSAGE? WHAT SPECIFIC ACTION STEPS CAN YOU TAKE THIS WEEK TO APPLY THIS PASSAGE?

WRITE A PRAYER OF RESPONSE TO YOUR STUDY OF GOD'S WORD.

Adore God for who He is, confess sins that He revealed in your own life, ask Him to empower you to walk in obedience, and pray for anyone who comes to mind as you study.

MIRACLES IN THE BOOK OF JOHN

Cana of Galilee — **1** — **TURNING WATER INTO WINE**
John 2:1-11 (Cana of Galilee)

From Galilee, healed the boy in Capernaum — **2** — **HEALING THE OFFICIAL'S SON**
John 4:43-54 (Galilee, but the boy was in Capernaum)

Jerusalem, by the Pool of Bethesda — **3** — **HEALING THE SICK**
John 5:1-9 (Jerusalem, by the Pool of Bethesda)

Across the Sea of Galilee, near Bethsaida — **4** — **THE FEEDING OF THE 5000**
John 6:1-15 (Across the Sea, near Bethsaida)

Sea of Galilee — **5** — **WALKING ON THE WATER**
John 6:16-25 (Sea of Galilee)

Jerusalem, near the Pool of Siloam — **6** — **HEALING THE BLIND MAN**
John 9:1-41 (Jerusalem, near the Pool of Siloam)

Bethany — **7** — **RAISING LAZARUS FROM THE DEAD**
John 11:1-44 (Bethany)

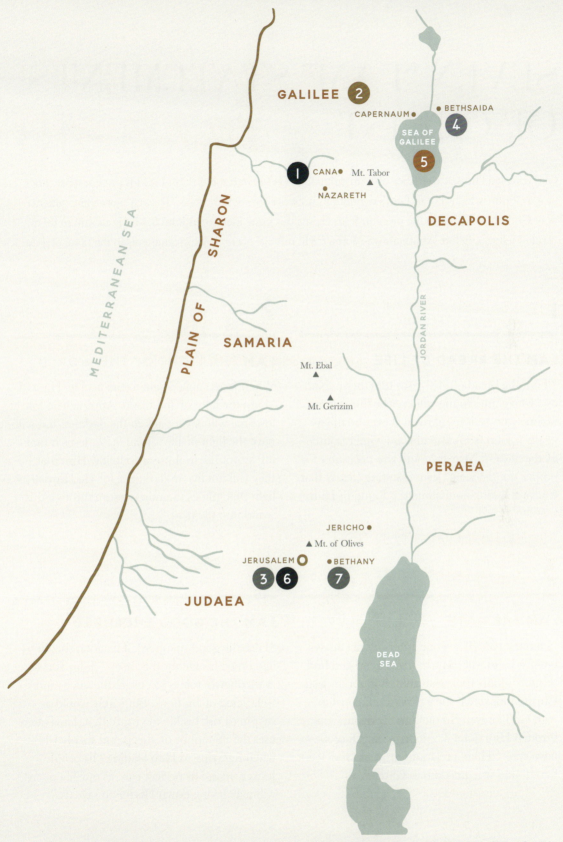

MIRACLES IN THE BOOK OF JOHN | 261

SEVEN "I AM" STATEMENTS OF CHRIST

God revealed Himself to Moses with an emphatic "I AM" in Exodus 3:14. I AM is present tense, not past or future, which reveals God's continuous presence through the ages. To each succeeding generation, God, the I AM, is in the present. Jesus claims this same identity in John 8:58: "Jesus said to them, 'Truly I tell you, before Abraham was, I am.'" He reveals seven "I Am" statements in the book of John.

1

I AM THE BREAD OF LIFE

"'I am the bread of life,' Jesus told them. 'No one who comes to me will ever be hungry, and no one who believes in me will ever be thirsty again'" (John 6:35). Bread was a vital resource of the ancient Near East and was necessary for proper nourishment. Jesus is stating clearly that true and lasting nourishment is found in Him.

2

I AM THE LIGHT OF THE WORLD

When Jesus spoke again to the people, He said, "I am the light of the world. Anyone who follows me will never walk in the darkness but will have the light of life" (John 8:12). Jesus is making a promise to those who follow Him that they will not live in darkness, for He Himself is light that guides them in wisdom through this world into the next.

3

I AM THE GATE

"I am the gate. If anyone enters by me, he will be saved and will come in and go out and find pasture" (John 10:9). Salvation is found in Jesus Christ alone. He is the gate to a relationship with God forever. No one can enter but through Him (John 3:3, John 14:6). Once we have entered into a relationship with God, we have found true freedom in Christ.

4

I AM THE GOOD SHEPHERD

"I am the good shepherd. The good shepherd lays down his life for the sheep" (John 10:11). A shepherd's role is to ensure the safety and well-being of his flock. But rarely would a shepherd risk his life to ensure that. Jesus often uses the metaphor of sheep and shepherd when referring to Him leading His people. Jesus reveals His perfect care as our Shepherd, willingly laying down His life to save us.

5

I AM THE RESURRECTION AND THE LIFE

"Jesus said to her, 'I am the resurrection and the life. The one who believes in me, even if he does, will live. Everyone who lives and believes in me will never die'" (John 11:25-26). Scripture says that whoever believes in Jesus would not perish but have eternal life (John 3:16). Jesus as the resurrection and the life brings life to the physically and spiritually dead! Even after our physical bodies reach their end, we still have life with Christ.

6

I AM THE WAY, THE TRUTH, AND THE LIFE

"Jesus told him, 'I am the way, the truth, and the life. No one comes to the Father except through me'" (John 14:6). There is no other way into a relationship with God except through salvation in Christ Jesus who paid the penalty for our sin and bore the wrath that we deserve. As Peter said, "There is salvation in no one else, for there is no other name under heaven given to people by which we must be saved" (Acts 4:12). Jesus is the only way to eternal life.

7

I AM THE VINE

"I am the vine; you are the branches. The one who remains in me and I in him produces much fruit, because you can do nothing without me" (John 15:5). Jesus is teaching us to remain in Him. When we abide in Him, we draw from His strength and wisdom, and we bear His fruit and flourish.

PASSION WEEK TIMELINE

SUNDAY
Jesus enters Jerusalem triumphantly — *John 12:12-19*
[CROSS REFERENCE]
MATTHEW 21:1-11, MARK 11:1-10, LUKE 19:29-44

TUESDAY
Jesus predicts His death and speaks of its significance — *John 12:20-50*

THURSDAY
The Last Supper — *John 13*
[CROSS REFERENCE]
MATTHEW 26:20, MARK 14:17, LUKE 22:14-16

Jesus comforts his disciples as they question the coming events — *John 14*
Jesus teaches that He is the true Vine — *John 15*
The promise of the Holy Spirit is given — *John 16*
Jesus' prayer in the garden of Gethsemane — *John 17*
Jesus is betrayed by Judas, and Peter denies Him — *John 18:1-27*
[CROSS REFERENCE]
MATTHEW 26:47-75, MARK 14:43-72, LUKE 22:47-62

FRIDAY
Jesus' trial where He is sentenced to death — *John 18:28–19:16*
[CROSS REFERENCE]
MATTHEW 17:11-26, MARK 15:1-15, LUKE 22:66-23:25

Jesus' crucifixion and burial — *John 19:17-42*
[CROSS REFERENCE]
MATTHEW 27:27-61, MARK 15:16-47, LUKE 23:26-56

SUNDAY
Jesus' resurrection and final word to His disciples — *John 20*
[CROSS REFERENCE]
MATTHEW 28, MARK 16, LUKE 24

JERUSALEM

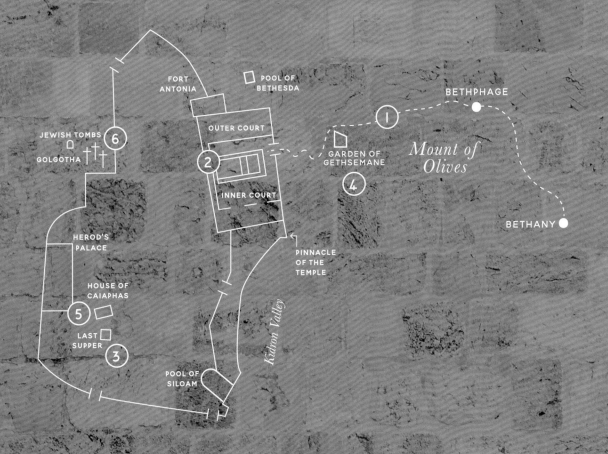

What is the Gospel?

THANK YOU FOR READING AND ENJOYING THIS STUDY WITH US! WE ARE ABUNDANTLY GRATEFUL FOR THE WORD OF GOD, THE INSTRUCTION WE GLEAN FROM IT, AND THE EVER-GROWING UNDERSTANDING IT PROVIDES FOR US OF GOD'S CHARACTER. WE ARE ALSO THANKFUL THAT SCRIPTURE CONTINUALLY POINTS TO ONE THING IN INNUMERABLE WAYS: THE GOSPEL.

We remember our brokenness when we read about the fall of Adam and Eve in the garden of Eden (Genesis 3), where sin entered into a perfect world and maimed it. We remember the necessity that something innocent must die to pay for our sin when we read about the atoning sacrifices in the Old Testament. We read that we have all sinned and fallen short of the glory of God (Romans 3:23) and that the penalty for our brokenness, the wages of our sin, is death (Romans 6:23). We all need grace and mercy, but most importantly, we all need a Savior.

We consider the goodness of God when we realize that He did not plan to leave us in this dire state. We see His promise to buy us back from the clutches of sin and death in Genesis 3:15. And we see that promise accomplished with Jesus Christ on the cross. Jesus Christ knew no sin yet became sin so that we might become righteous through His sacrifice (2 Corinthians 5:21). Jesus was tempted in every way that we are and lived sinlessly. He was reviled yet still yielded Himself for our sake, that we may have life abundant in Him. Jesus lived the perfect life that we could not live and died the death that we deserved.

The gospel is profound yet simple. There are many mysteries in it that we will never understand this side of heaven, but there is still overwhelming weight to its implications in this life. The gospel tells of our sinfulness and God's goodness and a gracious gift that compels a response. We are saved by grace through faith, which means that we rest with faith in the grace that Jesus Christ displayed on the cross (Ephesians 2:8-9). We cannot save ourselves from our brokenness or do any amount of good works to merit God's favor. Still, we can have faith that what Jesus accomplished in His death, burial, and resurrection was more than enough for our salvation and our eternal delight. When we accept God, we are commanded to die to ourselves and our sinful desires and live a life worthy of the calling we have received (Ephesians 4:1). The gospel compels us to be sanctified, and in so doing, we are conformed to the likeness of Christ Himself. This is hope. This is redemption. This is the gospel.

SCRIPTURES TO REFERENCE:

GENESIS 3:15	*I will put hostility between you and the woman, and between your offspring and her offspring. He will strike your head, and you will strike his heel.*
ROMANS 3:23	*For all have sinned and fall short of the glory of God.*
ROMANS 6:23	*For the wages of sin is death, but the gift of God is eternal life in Christ Jesus our Lord.*
2 CORINTHIANS 5:21	*He made the one who did not know sin to be sin for us, so that in him we might become the righteousness of God.*
EPHESIANS 2:8-9	*For you are saved by grace through faith, and this is not from yourselves; it is God's gift — not from works, so that no one can boast.*
EPHESIANS 4:1-3	*Therefore I, the prisoner in the Lord, urge you to walk worthy of the calling you have received, with all humility and gentleness, with patience, bearing with one another in love, making every effort to keep the unity of the Spirit through the bond of peace.*

THANK YOU FOR STUDYING GOD'S WORD WITH US!

CONNECT WITH US

@THEDAILYGRACECO

@DAILYGRACEPODCAST

CONTACT US

INFO@THEDAILYGRACECO.COM

SHARE

#THEDAILYGRACECO

VISIT US ONLINE

WWW.THEDAILYGRACECO.COM

MORE DAILY GRACE!

DAILY GRACE® PODCAST